Life, Literature, and Thought Library

ELIZABETHAN LYRICS

LIFE, LITERATURE, AND THOUGHT LIBRARY

General Editor
PROFESSOR VIVIAN DE SOLA PINTO, D.PHIL.
PROFESSOR OF ENGLISH IN THE UNIVERSITY OF NOTTINGHAM

ENGLISH BIOGRAPHY IN THE SEVENTEENTH CENTURY
VIVIAN DE SOLA PINTO, D.PHIL., *Professor of English, Nottingham*

A CHAUCER SELECTION
L. J. LLOYD, *Librarian of University College, Exeter*

GODWIN AND THE AGE OF TRANSITION
A. E. RODWAY, PH.D.

THE IDEA OF A LIBERAL EDUCATION
A Selection from the Works of Newman
HENRY TRISTRAM, B.LITT.

ENGLISH PASTORAL POETRY
From the Beginnings to Marvell
FRANK KERMODE, *Professor of English, Manchester*

ELIZABETHAN LYRICS
A Critical Anthology
KENNETH MUIR, *King Alfred Professor of English Literature, Liverpool*

THE PRE-RAPHAELITES IN LITERATURE AND ART
DENNIS WELLAND, *Lecturer in English, Nottingham*

SWIFT ON HIS AGE
Selected Prose and Verse
COLIN J. HORNE, *Professor of English, Adelaide*

A YOUTH LEANING AGAINST A TREE AMONG ROSES

Nicholas Hillyarde

Victoria and Albert Museum. Crown Copyright

Fr.

ELIZABETHAN LYRICS

A CRITICAL ANTHOLOGY

EDITED BY

KENNETH MUIR

King Alfred Professor of English Literature
in the University of Liverpool

GEORGE G. HARRAP & CO. LTD

LONDON TORONTO WELLINGTON SYDNEY

First published in Great Britain 1952
by George G. Harrap & Co. Ltd
182 High Holborn, London, W.C.1

Reprinted: 1958; 1960; 1961; 1962; 1966

Composed in Garamond type and printed by
Western Printing Services Ltd., Bristol
Made in Great Britain

FOREWORD

This series aims at presenting in an attractive form English texts which have not only intrinsic merit as literature, but which are also valuable as manifestations of the spirit of the age in which they were written. The plan was inspired by the desire to break away from the usual annotated edition of English classics and to provide a series of books illustrating some of the chief developments in English civilization since the Middle Ages. Each volume will have a substantial introduction, which will relate the author to the main currents of contemporary life and thought, and which will be an important part of the book. Notes, where given, will be brief, stimulating, and designed to encourage the spirit of research in the student. It is believed that these books will be of especial value to students in universities and the upper forms of schools, and that they will also appeal very much to the general reader.

VIVIAN DE SOLA PINTO
General Editor

PREFACE

THIS anthology, of which each section is arranged in roughly chronological order, attempts to give a representative selection of the Elizabethan lyrics, though some of the most famous, as they are easily accessible elsewhere, have been deliberately omitted. For reasons which will be apparent, poems have been included which were written either before or after the reign of Elizabeth.

As the Elizabethan age is still regarded by some historians as one of effortless spontaneity, and the lyric writers as a "nest of singing birds," I have tried to redress the balance by showing that their art was more important than their presumed spontaneity; and as Elizabethan sonneteers are sometimes blamed for their insincerity I have included a discussion of what constitutes poetic sincerity.

I am grateful to Mr Arthur Creedy for checking the texts of many of the poems, and to Mr Arnold Davenport for reading the introduction.

K. M.

CONTENTS

INTRODUCTION

CASTIGLIONE, in *The Courtier* (1528), which appeared in Hoby's translation in 1561, described the qualities a 'courtier' should possess. He should be of good birth and breeding, handsome, graceful, strong, courageous, a good performer in tournaments, fashionable in his dress, witty, prudent, temperate, upright, with charming manners, able to read Greek and Latin, to play a musical instrument, to sing, to draw, to appreciate painting, and to write both verse and prose when the occasion arose. Castiglione's book was popular in England, and, in the comparative calm of the Elizabethan settlement, it furnished a model of behaviour for the fashionable lover. The demand that the courtier, or lover, should be skilful at music and poetry had been fulfilled at the court of Henry VIII, and if it led to the writing of a great deal of indifferent poetry it at least ensured that poetry would be valued, and it provided an audience capable of appreciating the poetry of others.

Most of the lyrical poetry of the period is, in fact, love poetry; and good love poetry can be written only if there is approximate equality between the sexes. Women had been put on a pedestal by the courts of love in the middle ages, perhaps because of their actual subservience to men in ordinary society. But one of the effects of the Renaissance was to raise the position of women, so that in Shakespeare's comedies the heroines (Portia, Viola, Rosalinda) are more than equal to the men. In England, no doubt, the presence of a female sovereign and one who was the focus of patriotism and the object of flattery and adoration, assisted the general trend.

The Elizabethan lyric was partly a development of the medieval lyric, and some of the stanza-forms employed can be traced back to the time of Chaucer. Others are to be found in the court songs of Henry VIII's reign. But although the native influence should not be disregarded, the foreign influence was decisive. Italian, French, Latin, and Spanish poetry all contributed. From Italy came the sonnet form and many of the conventions to be found in Elizabethan love-poetry. The themes treated by Petrarch in his sonnets addressed to Laura—the transitoriness of beauty, the pains of absence, the immortality conferred by poetry, the cruelty and chastity of the lady—were echoed by countless English poets, either from the original Italian or from Petrarch's Italian and French imitators. Above all, the theme of unrequited love, which offered a more prolonged and dramatic subject than consummated love, became a favourite with English sonneteers. The French poets of the sixteenth century, Ronsard, Du Bellay, and Desportes in particular, were much imitated in England; and the pastoral tone of much lyric verse probably derived from French and Italian sources, and perhaps from the pastoral romance *Diana*, which —like Sidney's *Arcadia*—had lyrics interspersed. Ovid's influence was considerable on narrative poetry, and perceptible on lyrics; and Horace and Catullus were imitated by Campion, Jonson, and others.

Most of the lyrics in this anthology were written in the last fifteen years of the sixteenth century and the first twelve years of the seventeenth—roughly covering Shakespeare's working life; but one must go back to the reign of Henry VIII to find the seeds of this poetic harvest. The King himself composed both words and music of one or two tolerable songs; there was at least one good Court composer, Cornish; and many of the courtiers wrote songs. The music of these songs, however, is generally better than the words, and the movement would have had no literary importance if there had not been a poet of genius to take advantage of the situation. Sir Thomas Wyatt, a diplomat by profession, was introduced while abroad to French and Italian poetry, and his great achievement is to be found not so much in his direct translations and close adaptations of Petrarch and other poets, or even in his introduction of the sonnet, terza rima, and the rondeau into England, but in his fusion of foreign influence and native forms, of Italian conventions of love with individual feeling. Although many of his poems were apparently written to be sung, the best would have gained little from an accompaniment; and they may, indeed, have had none, for their colloquial rhythms seem to demand the speaking, rather than the singing, voice, and they made exquisite use of the tension between the two forms of verse available to the poet at the beginning of the sixteenth century.[1] Henry Howard, Earl of Surrey, looked to Wyatt as his master; but to turn from one poet to the other is like passing from Donne to Cowley or Waller. Surrey's verse is smooth and accomplished, but without the passionate ruggedness, the depth, and the cunning irregularities of Wyatt's.

When Wyatt died in 1542 and Surrey was executed a few years later, their work was still in manuscript, though Wyatt seems to have written an envoy for a projected volume of verse. It was not until the last year of Queen Mary's reign that Tottel printed a substantial selection of their poems as the chief contributions to *Songes and Sonettes*, which is generally regarded as the first of the Elizabethan miscellanies, though it was neither Elizabethan nor the first miscellany.[2]

MISCELLANIES

MOST of the authors included in *Songes and Sonettes* were dead, and the living were published without their knowledge. The other contributors, both quick and dead, limped far behind Wyatt and Surrey; and the work even of these poets was

[1] The kind of verse used by the song-writers, and what D. W. Harding calls "the pausing line compounded of dissimilar rhythmical units."

[2] A few of Wyatt's poems had been printed earlier in *The Courte of Venus*, and *A Boke of Balettes* contains a doubtful poem of his.

emended to comply with the editor's theories of correct versification. Surrey, who was naturally smooth, suffered comparatively little in the process, but Wyatt's verse was dreadfully mangled. One poem, "They flee from me" (No. 1 in this edition) appeared with alterations in nearly every line, and in this debased form it has appeared in all the standard anthologies. Textual accuracy was not much prized by the Elizabethans. Those who copied poems into their commonplace-books were often poets themselves, and they made 'improvements' or additions if they felt so inclined; and the editors of the miscellanies, who often relied on such unreliable transcripts, made their own alterations as well.

Tottel's collection was immensely popular, running through ten editions in thirty years,[1] and inspiring many similar, if inferior, collections. These included Edwardes' *Paradyse of Daynty Devices* (1576), Proctor's *Gorgious Gallery of Gallant Inventions* (1578), Robinson's *Handefull of Pleasant Delites* (1584), Breton's *Bowre of Delights* (1591), *The Phœnix Nest* (1593), *The Passionate Pilgrime* (1599), Bodenham's *Englands Helicon* (1600), and Davison's *Poetical Rapsody* (1602).[2]

These miscellanies are of several different kinds. Edwardes and Proctor, in spite of their promising titles, included much tedious moralizing and very little good poetry. Robinson compiled an anthology of popular ballads, unpretentious and often charming. *The Phœnix Nest* seems to have been written by a group of Oxford men, including such respectable poets as Ralegh, Greville, Lodge, and Greene. Bodenham restricted his choice to pastoral poetry: his standard was high, but nearly all of it had already appeared in print. Davison was at some

[1] Slender refers to the book in the first scene of *The Merry Wives of Windsor*. Shakespeare's most popular work, *Venus and Adonis*, which attracted by its 'daring' as much as by its poetical quality, also sold ten editions in thirty years.

[2] A few critics believe that Gascoigne wrote all *A Hundreth Sundrie Flowres* (1573), and Munday's *Banquet of Dainty Conceits* (1588) appears to be by a single author. Breton's name has been attached to several collections to which he was only the main contributor. Robinson's collection had appeared under another title in 1566, but no copy has survived.

pains to collect verse, much of it unpublished, and he included poems by himself and his brother.

As Sidney complained when he wrote his *Defence of Poesie*, there was a dearth of good poets between the death of Surrey and the publication of *The Shephards Caleneder* in 1579. Churchyard, Turberville, Googe, Howell, and even Gascoigne were (it must be confessed) a dull crowd; and for first-rate poetry one has to go to Sackville's superb contribution to *The Mirror for Magistrates* (1563). It was inevitable, therefore, that editors seeking to emulate Tottel between 1557 and 1579 should have had to fall back on more or less competent versifiers. Considering the reputation of Wyatt and Surrey, it is surprising that they had few real imitators: few sonnets were being written, and comparatively few love-poems. One poet, possibly Sir John Harington's father, competently translated a dozen of Petrarch's sonnets, but these remained in manuscript until the present century.[1] Many of the courtly poets, indeed, who were closer to Surrey in spirit, never underwent the 'stigma of print,'[2] and either because the compilers believed too narrowly that poetry ought to teach, or because the reading public genuinely preferred songs of good life to love-songs, the miscellanies in the early years of Elizabeth's reign were overpoweringly edifying.[3] The few poems chosen from these miscellanies are mercifully untypical of the general level of the contents, whereas there are so many good poems in the later miscellanies that it is impossible to include here all the ones worth reprinting.

Poets like Bolton, Breton, or the Davisons had no more in-

[1] *Cf.* K. Muir, "Sonnets from the Hill MS." (*Proceedings of the Leeds Philosophical and Literary Society*, 1950). Some of the verse of Wyatt's contemporaries and followers is reprinted in the same *Proceedings* (1947) as "Unpublished Poems from the Devonshire MS."

[2] *Cf.* the admirable article with this title by J. W. Saunders in *Essays in Criticism* (April 1951).

[3] The metrical version of the *Psalms* by Sternhold and Hopkins (1562) was a best-seller, perhaps because it was sung in church; but Tusser's *Five Hundreth Pointes of Good Husbandrie* was also a best-seller.

herent talent than Edwardes or Gascoigne, but on the whole they wrote better poetry. The explanation is to be found in the transformation of standards brought about by the example of Spenser and Sidney. After the publication of *The Shepheards Calender*, and still more after the publication of *The Faerie Queene* and *Astrophel and Stella*, even minor poets could be expected to display a sense of metrical form, and to avoid the crude devices which marred most of the lyrics written after the death of Surrey—long flabby lines, excessive alliteration, inappropriate diction, wooden rhythms—and though it might be complained of Spenser's imitators that "every warbler got his tune by heart," any tune is better than none. Much of the verse contained in the last three miscellanies represented here was no more than competent versifying; but it was at least competent, and the best poems have the inimitable freshness of a language first fully conscious of its powers.

SONNETS

In 1581 Penelope Devereux married Lord Rich, and Sidney, who might have married her at one time, fell in love only when she was out of his reach. This is the situation which occasioned the writing of *Astrophel and Stella*, though some of the earlier sonnets may have been written before 1581, and though Sidney may have expanded, as he certainly revised, the sequence after his own marriage in September 1583. The sonnets were not published until 1591, after the poet's death; but they circulated in more than one manuscript, and from one of these Newman got the copy for his piratical and inaccurate edition. Sidney had experimented with the sonnet form in his *Arcadia*, and his close friend Fulke Greville wrote some of his *Cælica* probably at the same time as Sidney was writing *Astrophel and Stella*. Another friend, Edmund Spenser, had translated some of Du Bellay's sonnets, though without rhyme, very early in his career; and some of the sonnets which were afterwards published in *Amoretti* (1595) may have been written much earlier. It was natural that Sidney and Spenser, who hoped to do for English poetry what Ronsard, Marot, and Du Bellay had done for French, should experiment in the sonnet form. Meanwhile Thomas Watson had published his *Hekatompathia* (1582), containing more than ninety eighteen-line poems, mostly translated from Italian sonnets; and John Soowthern, under the influence of Ronsard, had included thirteen (dreadfully clumsy) sonnets in his *Pandora* (1584). But in spite of these forerunners, it was undoubtedly Sidney's sequence which started the sonneteering craze; and the early practitioners were connected with the Sidney circle. Apart from Spenser and Greville, there was Samuel Daniel, some of whose sonnets were printed in the Newman edition, and who was a protégé of the Countess of Pembroke, Sidney's sister; and there was Henry Constable, who, even if he had not seen *Astrophel and Stella* in manuscript, was certainly acquainted with its author, and who also addressed a sonnet to Lady Rich.

In the years which followed the publication of *Astrophel and Stella* a large number of imitations appeared: in 1592 Daniel's *Delia* and Constable's *Diana*; in 1593 Lodge's *Phillis*, Watson's *Tears of Fancie*, Giles Fletcher's *Licia*, and Barnabe Barnes's *Parthenophil and Parthenophe*; in 1594 Percy's feeble *Coelia*, the anonymous *Zepheria*, and Drayton's first collection, *Ideas Mirrour*; in 1595 Spenser's *Amoretti*, Richard Barnfield's *Cynthia*, Barnes's *Divine Centurie of Spiritual Sonnets*, and Chapman's *Coronet for his Mistresse Philosophie*. These last two titles are the first examples of sequences not devoted to Petrarchan love, of which Constable's posthumously published *Spiritual Sonnets* is a fine early example and Donne's *Divine Sonnets* the culmination. In 1596 came three bad volumes, Griffin's *Fidessa*, Linche's *Diella*, and William Smith's *Chloris*; and in the following year Tofte's *Laura* brought the main harvest of sonnets to an inglorious end. But Drayton continued to write sonnets, his first notable ones appearing in the 1599 edition of

Idea, and his very best not until twenty years later. The craze spread to Scotland, where it inspired some sonnets by King James, as well as the *Aurora* of Sir William Alexander, and two volumes by William Drummond of Hawthornden (1616, 1623). Shakespeare's *Sonnets* (1609), one of the last collections to be published, may have been written fifteen or even twenty years before.[1] Finally came Greville's *Cælica* (1633), much of which had been written nearly half a century before, and Donne's *Divine Sonnets* (1633, 1635); and between these two dates there came the last belated sequence of love-sonnets, Habington's *Castara*.

A number of sonneteers have been omitted from this list, though some of those included are miserable poetasters. One volume, *Zepheria*, is so ludicrous that one would think it intentionally so if it had not been parodied:

> When I emprised, though in my love's affections,
> The silver lustre of thy brow to unmask,
> Though hath my muse hyperbolised trajections;
> Yet stands it, aye, deficient to such task.
>
> 'Mongst Delian Nymphs, in Angel's University,
> Thou, my Zepheria, liv'st matriculated.

Sir John Davies wrote a series of gulling sonnets, and his parody of *Zepheria* is less ridiculous than the original.[2] His most effective counterblast is the following, which is apparently not aimed at any particular poet:

> The Lover under burthen of his Mistress' love,
> Which like to Ætna did his heart oppress,
> Did give such pitious groans that he did move
> The heav'ns at length to pity his distress;

[1] Hotson, *Shakespeare's Sonnets Dated*, argues that they were all written by 1590, but the view has not met with general acceptance.

[2] Perhaps Sir John Davies was the author of *Zepheria*, it being intended as a parody.

> But for the fates in their high court above
> Forbade to make the grievous burthen less,
> The gracious powers did all conspire to prove
> If miracle this mischief might redress.
> Therefore regarding that the load was such
> As no man might with one man's might sustain,
> And that mild patience imported much
> To him that should endure an endless pain.
> By their decree he soon transformed was
> Into a patient burden-bearing Ass.

Davies was satirizing what he called "the bastard sonnets of these rhymers base," rather than the convention in which nearly all the sonnets were written; and he himself used the convention seriously, but ineffectively, in a series published in *A Poetical Rapsody*. Other writers, however, attacked the convention itself. Romeo, at the beginning of the play, is conventionally in love with the scornful Rosaline, and he has all the usual symptoms of the unrequited lover. Later on, when he has fallen in love with Juliet, Mercutio, who is unaware that Rosaline has been displaced in his affections, exclaims:

> Now is he for the numbers that Petrarch flow'd in; Laura, to his lady, was a kitchen-wench—marry; she had a better love to berhyme her; Dido, a dowdy; Cleopatra, a gipsy; Helen and Hero, hildings and harlots; Thisbe, a gray eye or so, but not to the purpose.

In fact, as Mercutio discovers, Romeo is now witty and sociable instead of maudlin and affected. The scornful mistress is satirized in *As You Like It*, and Benedick baits Claudio when he falls in love much as Mercutio rags Romeo. In his own *Sonnets*, Shakespeare criticizes the conventions even while he employs them:

> So is it not with me as with that Muse,
> Stirr'd by a painted beauty to his verse;
> Who heaven itself for ornament doth use,
> And every fair with his fair doth rehearse . . .

O, let me, true in love, but truly write,
  And then believe me, my love is as fair
As any mother's child, though not so bright
  As those gold candles fix'd in heaven's air.
(No. 21)

My mistress' eyes are nothing like the sun;
  Coral is far more red than her lips' red;
If snow be white, why then her breasts are dun;
  If hairs be wires, black wires grow on her head . . .

  And yet, by heaven, I think my love as rare
  As any she belied with false compare.
(No. 130)

The Princess, in *Love's Labour's Lost*, similarly objects to Boyet's flattery:

my beauty, though but mean,
Needs not the painted flourish of your praise.
Beauty is bought by judgement of the eye,
Not utter'd by base sale of chapmen's tongues;
I am less proud to hear you tell my worth
Then you much willing to be counted wise
In spending your wit in the praise of mine.

It was Shakespeare's consciousness of the artificiality and insin-cerity of the fashionable sonnet that enabled him to give the impression of truth; his praise seems almost to be dragged from him against his will.

Many other attacks on the conventions of the sonneteers might be quoted. It was a favourite topic of the satirists and of the writers of conversation manuals. Florio, for example, in *Second Fruites*, wrote of

> Some more active gallants made of a finer mould, by devising how to win their Mistress's favours, and how to blaze and blanch their passions, with æglogues, Songs, and Sonnets, in pitiful verse or miserable prose, and most for a fashion.

Florio's opponent, John Eliot, in his *Ortho-Epia Gallica*, has an amusing account of a certain Jeronimo Pierruche, who was

> Cherry-cheeked, fair and well-liking, merry, with a slick face, pleasant-disposed, and a tratling companion . . . Now he is lean, wan, pale, looking like one half dead, weak, ugly, dreaming, loving to be alone, and cares for nobody's company: so that none of those that had seen him before, could now know him again . . . Now he is mad: he is foolish: oftentimes he walketh alone: but will never speak to anybody: always mumbling or recording something in English verse, that he hath made to his sweetheart and minion. One while you shall see him feign a sea of tears, a lake of miseries, wring his hands and weep, accuse the heaven, curse the earth, make an anatomy of his heart, to freeze, to burn, to adore, to play the idolator, to admire, to feign heavens, to forge hells, to counterfeit Sisyphus, to play the Tantalus, to represent Titius' Tragedy. And by and by he exalteth in his verses that Diana whom he loveth best; her hair is nothing but gold wire, her brows arches and vaults of Ebenus: her eyes twinkling stars like Castor and Pollux, her looks lightnings: her mouth coral; her neck orient pearl: her breath balm, amber, and musk: her throat of snow: her neck milk-white: her dugs that she hath on her breast, mountains or apples of alabaster. All the rest of her body is but a prodigality and treasure of heaven and of nature that she had reserved to work the perfection of his mistress and dear . . . . O the poor passionate is cruelly eclipsed! One while you shall see him drowned in tears and lamentations, to make the air echo with his sighs, complaints, murmurings, rages, imprecations: otherwhiles if he have got but a glance of his goddess, you shall see him cross, pass and repass five or six times a day through a street that he may have but one friendly look of her eye that he loveth best.

A more serious attack on the convention had been made by Giordano Bruno in his *De Gli eroici furori*—a work which has been translated as *The Heroic Enthusiasts*—which he dedicated to Sidney in 1585. In the dedication the famous philosopher attacked Petrarchism and the worship of women; and though he exempted Englishwomen from his criticisms, and even paid a compliment to Stella, he strongly disapproved of the craze which had swept Italy and France, and was about to sweep England. It has been suggested that Berowne's speech of retraction,[1] in which he argues that love is a liberal education, was Shakespeare's reply to Bruno's attack.

There was plenty of justification for the contemporary criticisms of the sonneteers. In order to appreciate the best Elizabethan sonnets, it is necessary to recognize that many of them are bad, and that most of them are little more than competent poetic exercises. Lynch, Smith, Tofte, and Percy have little to recommend them; Lodge, Barnes, and Fletcher are totally lacking in originality; and even some of the greater sonneteers are very uneven. All Drayton's early sonnets are pedestrian, and he rose to greatness only in his old age; Daniel is lacking in passion; and if Spenser maintains a high level of melody and craftsmanship, not one of his sonnets can be put in the first rank. We are left with much of *Astrophel and Stella*, nearly all Shakespeare's *Sonnets*, and occasional successes of Drayton, Daniel, Constable, and a few other poets.

The question of the sincerity of Elizabethan sonnets has aroused a great deal of barren controversy. It was not difficult for critics to show that many of the sonnets were direct translations from the French or Italian, that many others were suggested by foreign originals both in choice of theme and in details of treatment, and that English poets copied from each other as well as from Petrarch and Desportes. It is clear, moreover, that the sonnets were written within a particular convention; and therefore, it is argued, they cannot express real feeling. Sir Sidney Lee, after pointing out parallels between Sidney and Petrarch, came to the odd conclusion that

> detachment from the realities of passion, which comes of much reading about love in order to write about it, is the central feature of Sidney's sonnets.

[1] See *Love's Labour's Lost*, IV, iii, 285 ff. *Cf.* F. Yates, *A Study of Love's Labour's Lost* (Cambridge University Press, 1936).

Sidney himself complained in his *Defence of Poesie* of the unreality of contemporary love-poetry:

> But truly many of such writings, as come under the banner of unresistable love, if I were a mistress, would never persuade me they were in love: so coldly they apply fiery speeches, as men that had rather read lovers' writings, and so caught up certain swelling phrases, which hang together like a man that once told my father the wind was a North-west, and by South, because he would be sure to name winds enough, than that in truth they feel those passions, which easily as I think may be bewraied by that same forcibleness or *energia* (as the Greeks call it) of the writer.

From this it would seem that Sidney wished the love-poet to be genuinely in love, or at least to give that illusion to his readers; and it is obvious that he was not guilty of the faults he condemns in others. In *Astrophel and Stella* he was continually protesting his sincerity, that he was "no pick-purse of another's wit," that he was not one of Pindar's apes, nor one of those

> that poor Petrarch's long-deceased woes,
> With new-born sighs and denizen'd wit do sing.

He wrote to "ease a burthened heart"; and his recipe for poetic composition was to look in his heart and write. Lee could claim that such protestations were not without parallels in earlier poets, and that Sidney was being as imitative in them as in the rest of his sequence. But the fact that Sidney had read Petrarch and Ronsard—which nobody denies—does not mean that his love was purely, or even mainly, fictional. When he fell in love with Stella after her marriage he must have been aware that he was in the traditional Petrarchan situation; and since he was not writing his autobiography but creating a work of art, he was not bound to be biographically accurate. In all poetry there is an element of dramatization, and Sidney may well have imagined himself and Stella in invented situations. Perhaps he never saw Stella on the Thames, and it may be that he composed his sonnets on the subject because Petrarch had written addresses to the Po and the Rhône, though his sonnet is totally different from either of Petrarch's. No poet is under oath; but that there was a basis of fact in Sidney's sequence it would be unreasonable to deny. There is no real doubt that most of the sonnets were written to Penelope Devereux after her marriage to Lord Rich, that they accurately reflect a real conflict in Sidney's mind, and that some of the sonnets and interspersed songs were based on actual incidents.[1]

Lady Sidney's later friendship with Lady Rich, who was by that time her sister-in-law, does not prove that Sidney never made love to her, as some critics naïvely suppose, but merely that Lady Sidney was a sensible woman. If poet's wives refused to speak with every woman to whom their husbands had written poems they would drastically limit their acquaintance; and Stella had, after all, refused to grant Astrophel's suit.[2]

Less is known about the circumstances of the other sonnet-sequences. As Spenser's *Amoretti* were published with the poem which avowedly celebrates his own marriage to Elizabeth Boyle, and as one of the sonnets mentions her by name, it is natural to assume that the whole sequence was dedicated to her, even if it was not all inspired by her. The sonnets were probably arranged so as to form a kind of story. No one has yet identified Daniel's Delia satisfactorily, though some have supposed her to be the Countess of Pembroke, who, like Delia, lived near the Wiltshire Avon. Some of the sonnets were originally addressed to a golden-haired woman; and the fact that Daniel afterwards substituted "sable" for "golden" in two of them suggests that one at least of his mistresses was not imaginary. Not that it matters: for his sonnets are more concerned with the

[1] The song given as No. 187 in this edition, for example.

[2] Penelope refused Sidney because she was in love with Mountjoy, not from chastity. G. M. Matthews, however (*Essays in Criticism*, II, ii, p. 127), argues that the Sonnets imply that Penelope became Sidney's mistress, and that she was not in love with Mountjoy until after Sidney's death.

destruction of beauty by time than with the love of a particular woman. We know rather more about the heroine of Drayton's *Idea*, Anne Goodere. The poet had been educated, and had served as a page, in her father's house. There are references to her in his letters as well as in his verse, and Drayton continued to write sonnets to her after her marriage to Sir Henry Rainsford. He became a devoted friend of the family, and wrote an elegy on Sir Henry's death. That Lady Rainsford deserved the devotion of the poet, who loved her for nearly half a century, can be inferred from an unprofessional note in the casebook of Dr Hall, Shakespeare's son-in-law, referring to her loveliness when she was long past her prime.

The identity of Mr W. H., of the Rival Poet, and of the Dark Lady of Shakespeare's *Sonnets* is still a matter of controversy, which is unlikely to be settled by Dr Leslie Hotson's new candidates for the rôles. Lee thought that the story must have been invented, because it would otherwise reveal "moral instability" in the author. It almost looks as though Lee's industrious researches into the sources of Elizabethan sonnets, and his belief that Sidney was unacquainted with love, were really due to his desire to safeguard Shakespeare's moral reputation. The odd thing is that he would rather have believed that Shakespeare wrote affectionate sonnets to wheedle money out of a patron than that he meant what he said.

Perhaps the greatest argument against the sonnets' being pure fiction is that one would expect in that case a tidier, more coherent story; and, as there would be no objection to publishing them if they were fiction, Shakespeare would surely have prepared them for the press as he had done his narrative poems. As fiction the sequence is confused, obscure, and badly arranged. On the other hand, if the sonnets were written to please a patron one wonders whether Shakespeare were wise to indulge in irony at his patron's expense, and to publicize his not very elevated conduct.

Not that the 'sincerity' of poetry depends on its biographical truth. A sonnet-sequence could be poetically sincere, even though the events described in it were totally imaginary. In such a case the poet would be attempting to tell the truth about some aspect of love, not by universalizing his own experience, but by invention, or by the imitation of previous poets. The results would probably not be good unless the poet had at some time been in love; but one has only to think of speeches put into the mouths of Shakespeare's characters to realize that what outside a play might be branded as a poetic exercise, not expressing the poet's immediate and personal feelings, may convey the illusion of real passion more conclusively than the heartfelt verses of lesser poets. On the whole, perhaps, the lyric poets of the sixteenth century were less personal than the great Romantics, but they were not necessarily less sincere.

It must be admitted that the greater sonneteers are more original than the smaller fry. Greville imitates Sidney in a few poems, but no sources have been discovered for most of his sonnets. None of Sidney's sonnets is a mere imitation of a foreign original; and, as Professor Renwick has pointed out

> The Petrarchan convention was so universally accepted all over western Europe that nothing is easier than to collect 'parallels' and nothing more difficult than to fix upon 'sources.'

Only two of Shakespeare's sonnets, and those possibly spurious, have been traced to a definite source, though in a few (*e.g.* "Not marble nor the gilded monuments" and "Like as the waves made towards the pibled shore") he writes variations on Latin themes. Spenser, to quote Renwick again,

> rarely takes more than a hint. Even where he begins from another man's work he seldom fails to give it a new turn, either original or by combination with another commonplace.

But a large number of sonnets by other Elizabethan poets were imitations, or even translations, of French and Italian sonnets. Lodge translated from Ariosto, Ronsard, Desportes, and others; and Fletcher based twenty-three of his sonnets on

Angerianus, and sixteen on other poets. These are extreme cases. More characteristic are the borrowings of Daniel and Drayton. Eighteen sonnets in *Delia* and sixteen in *Idea* were suggested by previous poets; but generally speaking these were adaptations, rather than translations, and often the hint was slight. One example must suffice. Daniel's best-known sonnet (No. 48 in this edition) is derived from Desportes, we are assured; but the only lines he echoes are the following:

> *Sommeil, paisible fils de la nuict solitaire . . .*
> *O frère de la mort, que tu m'es ennemy!*

Perhaps, too, *care-charmer* may have been derived from *chasse-soin*, which Lee declares was a favourite epithet of the French sonneteers. But this is hardly enough evidence on which to base a charge of plagiarism.

It is important to realize, however, that though servile imitation without individuality was condemned by Elizabethan critics, they held "the classical doctrine that originality of real worth is to be achieved only through creative imitation."[1] Soowthern and Lodge were attacked for their wholesale plagiarism, but Wyatt was not blamed for his versions of Petrarch.

Imitation can, of course, lead to mere pastiche; but great poets are often most truly original when they are most indebted. No one imagines that Prospero's farewell to his art is any the worse for being an inspired paraphrase of Ovid's *Metamorphoses*. We cannot possibly say that Elizabethan poets were insincere because they were conventional, for all poetry is conventional in one way or another; and, moreover, the actual

[1] Harold Ogden White, *Plagiarism and Imitation During the English Renaissance* (Harvard University Press, 1935), p. 202. It may be worth mentioning that poets, until the middle of the eighteenth century, had no feeling that it was wrong to imitate or echo previous poets. Thomas Gray, for example, calls the reader's attention to the origin of some of his phrases; and Pope printed the original Latin beside his imitations of Horace. But, at the end of the nineteenth century, imitation came to be regarded as little better than plagiarism, and to be treated with equal obloquy. It is only fair to Lee to say that when he dealt with the influence of Ovid on Shakespeare and the other Elizabethans he seems to have been aware that one could imitate creatively.

forms taken by love in a society are very much influenced by the books, paintings, plays, and films popular in that society. When gentlemen are supposed to prefer blondes they tend to fall in with the fashion; and brunettes, fearing that they may cease to attract, have recourse to the peroxide bottle. In the same way, in Shakespeare's time, when every educated man had read Petrarch and Du Bellay, their love was coloured by their reading, and the behaviour of their mistresses was affected by their expectations. When lovers wrote sonnets, or when poets impersonated lovers, it is not surprising that they should at the same time express their genuine and personal feelings and also produce sonnets not unlike the ones they had admired.[1]

But when all is said it is remarkable that so many poets, writing in a fashionable convention and imitating each other as well as foreign poets, should produce sonnet-sequences so varied in tone and style, and so completely distinguishable from each other. Sidney is one of the greatest of love-poets, and his anaylsis of love in what Nashe called his 'tragi-comedy of love performed by starlight' is in its way as realistic as Donne's. His colloquial and passionate style is totally different from the decorative and musical meditations of Spenser's *Amoretti*; and both again are different from Daniel's laments for the passing of beauty. Constable's love-sonnets are fashionable, clever, and ultimately unsatisfying; but the best of his religious sonnets are some of the most undervalued poems of the period. Greville seems to have been born middle-aged, and his good love-poems are few in number; but when in the middle of *Cælica* he turned to religious and philosophical themes his ruggedness and honesty triumph over his indifferent ear and his lack of sensuous awareness. Drayton's early sonnets have all the faults that one expects in a bad imitator of an effete trad-

[1] If we go to the Lake District we look at the scenery through Wordsworth's eyes. If we had been born three hundred years ago we should never have wanted to climb a mountain; and if we had been in the neighbourhood we should have had none of the exalted feelings that even the tourist now experiences as a matter of course.

tion; but as he approached middle age he learned to put more and more of himself into his verse, until, paradoxically, under the influence of Shakespeare, he abandoned the artificialities of his early style and achieved the summit of his career as a poet in what Elton called that 'wonderful dry-eyed sonnet,' "Since there's no help" (No. 69 in this edition).

The greatest of the sonneteers was Shakespeare; but it is important to emphasize that his sonnets depend for part of their effect on the tradition in which they were written, on the consummate expression of the great commonplaces, on the subtle deviations from the conventional, on the amalgam of tradition and the individual talent. Nearly all the themes on which he writes had been treated by other poets; but he is continually correcting the convention by the realities of his own experience. Although he consciously echoes Ovid he had proved upon his pulses the bitter conflict between time and beauty; and his faith that love can defy time impresses the reader with its truth because it was achieved only after a prolonged struggle. The sonnets have an extraordinary range. Although they are nearly all nominally love poems, they deal with friendship, with idealistic worship of beauty, with the sacrifice of friendship to love, with sensuality and lust, and sometimes with ideas and feelings about life to which love is merely a background. Some of the sonnets are witty—even bawdy—and several are ironical: all display a psychological realism and a depth of self-analysis which reveal the born dramatist, what Keats called "the mighty poet of the human heart." From the point of view of musical range they are unequalled even by Spenser; they are filled with vivid and original imagery, not all drawn from nature; and, as Mr Empson has shown,[1] many of them are much more subtle and complex than they appear on the surface. All the other Elizabethan sonnet-sequences appear insubstantial and 'literary' beside Shakespeare's, and only Sidney's approaches it in veri-

[1] In *Seven Types of Ambiguity* (Chatto and Windus, 1930).

similitude. Too much discussion of the identity of Mr W. H. and the rival poet has done Shakespeare a disservice, for we can never know how much of the story was experienced in real life and how much was invented, and such discussion has too often taken place of critical appreciation of the sonnets as poetry.

Donne's sonnets are strictly outside the period, but they are in a sense the culmination of Elizabethan religious sonnets. Barnes, Constable, Greville, and Drummond had all written on religious themes, and one of Shakespeare's greatest sonnets is an address to his soul; but only in Donne's *Divine Sonnets* do we get the realities of spiritual conflict in all their immediacy.

A word may be said on the form of the Elizabethan sonnet. The normal Petrarchan sonnet rhymes *abbaabbacdecde*; but Petrarch himself has six sonnets in quatrains, the first two linked by common rhymes (*ababababcdcede*) and several other variations. Sidney usually limited himself to five rhymes, and Spenser adopted the form *ababbcbccdcdee*. Constable follows the Petrarchan octave, but usually concludes his sonnets with a couplet. Drayton and Daniel both use the Shakespearian form (*ababcdcdefefgg*); Barnes uses this in his love-sonnets, but reverts to the Petrarchan form in his religious sonnets. The form employed influences the way a subject is treated. The Petrarchan sonnet usually has a break after the octave; but the poets who use the Shakespearian form usually, but not always, have three parallel statements in the quatrains, clinched by the final couplet.

POEMS FROM ROMANCES

As early as 1580 novelists began to insert poems into their tales, influenced either by the manuscript of Sidney's *Arcadia* or by foreign fiction. It became part of the recognized formula employed by Greene and Lodge, though not by Lyly. Most of this verse is pastoral in tone; but it is important to distinguish between the verse eclogues, the singing matches, and the poems supposed to be written by the characters in some of the romances, and the songs which are merely supposed to be sung, not composed, by one of the characters. Most of the good poems in the romances come in the second of these categories.

Many of the poems can be detached from their context without loss either to the poem or to the story; and some authors may have found this a convenient way of publishing their lyrical verse. Others cannot be detached at all, because they are essential to the story, and are meaningless apart from the story. Others, again, can be published separately, though they may thus lose some of their point. Sephestia's song (No. 94), for example, should really be read in its context:

> Menaphon having ended his roundelay, rising up, thinking to pass from the mountain down to the valley, casting his eye to the sea side, espied certain fragments of a broken ship floating upon the waves, and sundry persons driven upon the shore with a calm, walking all wet and weary upon the sands, wondering at this strange sight he stood amazed; yet desirous to see the event of this accident, he shrouded himself to rest unespied till he might perceive what would happen. At last he might descry it was a woman holding a child in her arms, and an old man directing her, as it were her guide. These three (as distressed wracks) preserved by some further forepointing fate, coveted to climb the mountain, the better to use the favour of the Sun, to dry their drenched apparel; at last crawled up where poor Menaphon lay close, and resting them under a bush, the old man did nothing but send out sighs, and the woman ceased not from streaming forth rivulets of tears, hung on her cheeks like the drops of pearled dew upon the riches of Flora. The poor babe was the touchstone of his mother's passions; for when he smiled and lay laughing in her lap, were her heart never so deeply overcharged with her present sorrows, yet kissing the pretty infant, she lightened out smiles from those cheeks, that were furrowed with continual sources of tears; but if he cried, then sighs as smokes, and sobs as thundercracks, foreran those showers, that with redoubled distress distilled from her eyes. Thus with pretty inconstant passions trimming up her

baby, and at last to lull him asleep, she warbled out of her woeful breast this ditty.

Lodge sometimes used verse as an integral part of the story, as in the wooing eclogue between Rosalynde and Rosader; and he made some distinction between the sophisticated songs of the gentry and the rude songs of the Shepherd Coridon; but some of the best songs can be detached from their contexts.

On the whole it must be admitted that the poems in the novels of the period are the most disappointing branch of Elizabethan lyric writing. Their range is limited, and the treatment is seldom individualized. Even Sidney's poems interspersed in *Arcadia* are lacking in the power and individuality displayed in *Astrophel and Stella*, partly, no doubt, because he was serving his apprenticeship as a poetic craftsman.

Sidney wrote originally to please a narrow circle. Greene wrote his novels as pot-boilers; but that he nevertheless achieved some of his best effects by taking pains can be seen from the song in *Penelope's Web*, a variation on a theme of Ariosto which he afterwards condensed into Maesia's song (No. 99):

The stately state that wise men count their good:
  The chiefest bliss that lulls asleep desire,
Is not descent from Kings and princely blood:
  Ne stately crown ambition doth require.
For birth by fortune is abased down,
And perils are compris'd within a crown.

The sceptre and the glittering pomp of mace,
  The head impal'd with honour and renown,
The kingly throne, the seat and regal place,
  Are toys that fade when angry fortune frown.
Content is far from such delights as those,
Whom woe and danger do envy as foes.

The cottage seated in the hollow dale,
  That fortune never fears, because so low:
The quiet mind that want doth set to sale,
  Sleeps safe when Princes' seats do overthrow.
Want smiles secure, when princely thoughts do feel
That fear and danger tread upon their heel.

Bless fortune, thou whose frown hath wrought thy good:
  Bid farewell to the crown that ends thy care.
The happy fates thy sorrows have withstood,
  By 'signing want and poverty thy share.
For now content (fond fortune to despite)
With patience 'lows thee quiet and delight.

This is a competent treatment of one of the favourite Elizabethan commonplaces which recurs again and again in Shakespeare's Histories; but Greene greatly improves on this poem by condensing its four stanzas into the two of Maesia's song.

SONGS FROM PLAYS

Some of the earliest English comedies include songs as an integral part of the entertainment: *Ralph Roister Doister*, performed by schoolboys, contains several, and *Gammer Gurton's Needle* the famous "Back and side go bare":

I cannot eat but little meat,
  My stomach is not good;
But sure I think that I can drink
  With him that wears a hood.
Though I go bare, take ye no care
  I nothing am a-cold;
I stuff my skin so full within
  Of jolly good ale and old.
Back and side go bare, go bare;
  Both foot and hand go cold;
But, belly, God send thee good ale enough.
  Whether it be new or old.

Many of the early Elizabethan plays, such as Pickering's *Horestes* (1567), Philip's *Patient Grissell* (1570), and R. B.'s *Apius and Virginia* (1575), also contains songs of some merit. Even before the advent of the great Elizabethan composers, singing was a popular pastime; and dramatists who sought to hold a mirror up to nature naturally included songs in their plays. Lyly, the first of the University Wits, who wrote his plays for the children of St Paul's choir school, had expert singers at his service, and he made great use of them. All his plays depend for part of their effect on his use of songs for one or more voices. Unfortunately, the songs were not printed in the early quartos, and they make their first appearance in the collected edition of 1632. Lyly had been dead for twenty-five years by this time, and it has been argued on the evidence of parallels that the editor, Blount, employed Dekker and Middleton to supply the missing songs. One can only say that the songs are exquisitely adapted to their contexts in Lyly's plays—more so, indeed, than parallel songs are adapted to their contexts in the plays of Dekker and Middleton. The original songs, if these are not the original ones, cannot have been very different in tone. In any case, Lyly's plays offer quite the best early example of the dramatic use of song. Many of the songs, indeed, resemble arias, duets, and trios from operatic works. In *Endimion*, for example, the three pages agree to sing in order to awaken the sleeping Sir Tophas, and their song is appropriately about his lady-love, Dipsas. Later in the play the same pages have another song, with plenty of stage business, with the constable and the watch. A third song, of the fairies, is also an integral part of the play, and would mean very little divorced from its context. During the singing of the song the fairies pinch Corsites and kiss Endymion:

Ombes. Pinch him, pinch him, black and blue!
Saucy mortals must not view
What the Queen of Stars is doing,
Nor pry into our fairy wooing.

1 *Fairy*. Pinch him blue
2 *Fairy*. And pinch him black.
3 *Fairy*. Let him not lack
Sharp nails to pinch him blue and red,
Till sleep has rock'd his addle-head.
4 *Fairy*. For the trespass he hath done,
Spots o'er all his flesh shall run.
Kiss Endymion, kiss his eyes,
Then to our midnight heidegyes.

n the nightingale song in *Campaspe* (Act V) the theme is carefully prepared by the preceding dialogue:

yl. Now shall you hear the third, who sings like a nightingale.
Diog. I care not: for I have heard a nightingale to sing herself.
yl. Sing, sirrha!

Trico thereupon sings this song:[1]

What bird so sings, yet so does wail?
Oh, 'tis the ravish'd nightingale.
Jug, jug, jug, jug, tereu, she cries,
And still her woes at midnight rise.

[1] Dekker's song in *The Sun's Darling* (pub. 1656) is clearly echoed from this oem, if it is not the original of it:

What bird so sings, yet so does wail?
'Tis Philomel the Nightingale;
Jugg, jugg, jugg, Tereu, she cries,
And hating earth, to heaven she flies.
Cuckoo.
Ha, ha, hark, hark, the cuckoos sing
Cuckoo to welcome in the spring.
Brave prick-song; who is't now we hear!
'Tis the lark's silver leer-a-leer:
Chirrup, the sparrow flies away;
For he fell to't ere break of day.
Cuckoo
Ha, ha, hark, hark, the cuckoos sing
Cuckoo, to welcome in the spring.

This would appear to be a garbled version of the other song, perhaps, altered fit a particular tune. The term 'prick-song' is more applicable to the nightgale than to the cuckoo or the lark, and the nightingale does not fly to heaven the lark may be described as doing. Shakespeare's "Hark! Hark! the lark" 609) may owe something to Lyly's song; but *The Sun's Darling* was not licensed r performance until long after Shakespeare's death.

Brave prick-song! Who is't now we hear?
None but the lark so shrill and clear;
How at heaven's gates she claps her wings,
The morn not waking till she sings.
Hark, hark, with what a pretty throat
Poor Robin red-breast tunes his note;
Hark how the jolly cuckoos sing
Cuckoo, to welcome in the spring,
Cuckoo, to welcome in the spring.

Dekker wrote a number of charming songs, but two that are usually ascribed to him (Nos. 124 and 125 in this edition), are possibly by Chettle. In an age when plays were frequently written in collaboration by two or more dramatists, it is virtually impossible to be certain of the authorship of many of the songs. Sometimes a song would be borrowed from another play. All the better dramatists, except Marlowe, Kyd, Chapman, and Tourneur, wrote excellent songs for their plays, though they are seldom so perfectly adapted to the scenes in which they appear as are those in Lyly's comedies.

Shakespeare's consummate use of song has been well analysed in Mr Richmond Noble's book.[1] Not only is every song perfect of its kind, but, with few exceptions, they could not be transferred from one play to another without spoiling their effect. It is sometimes possible to absorb the peculiar tone and atmosphere of a play from the songs alone. Ariel's songs create the magic atmosphere of *The Tempest* as surely as Stephano's drunken song creates the atmosphere of the scene in which he appears. The greenwood becomes real to us in *As You Like It* by means of the songs of Amiens and the pages. The haunting loveliness, tinged with melancholy, which critics have seen as the prevailing atmosphere of *Twelfth Night*, is derived partly from Feste's songs, and he has a genius for fitting his songs to his immediate audience. "Come away, come away

[1] *Shakespeare's Use of Song* (Oxford University Press, 1923).

death" would not suit Sir Toby; and "O mistress mine" would be poorly received by Orsino.

Shakespeare brilliantly avoids the besetting fault of the pastoral song, tepid unreality, by the clarity of his images and the sudden earthiness of his diction. Mr Bethell has pointed out,[1] for example, how Autolycus's songs are redeemed from the pastoral illusion by the use of such slangy, almost sordid, words as *doxy*, *aunt*, *pugging*, and *tumbling*. An equal freedom from illusion is to be found in the songs that close one of Shakespeare's early comedies, *Love's Labour's Lost*. In one, the cuckoo mocks married men with the immemorial gibe of cuckoldom; in the other, we have a realistic winter-piece, with coughing in the unheated church and Marian's nose unbeautifully red and raw.

A few songs have been included from Jacobean masques. In them, for the average spectator, the words were less important than the spectacle, the dancing, and the music; and only in the belated *Comus* does the poetry become more important than the accessories. But Jonson and Campion, in spite of the cramping nature of the form, contrived to write some beautiful lyrics. Most of them, however, lose much of their point when they are detached from their contexts.

MADRIGALS AND AIRS

THE age of Shakespeare was also the golden age of English music. Not only were there several great composers, but musical culture was widely diffused. The habit of singing part-songs in middle-class homes was widespread; the upper classes had their own professional musicians. The Elizabethans believed that the best servants sang at their work, and they would often choose them for their musical accomplishments, either as players or singers, so that they could take part with the family in musical evenings. Manual workers, shoemakers, tinkers, tailors, and sailors all sang at their work; and Dekker's *Shoe-*

[1] In *The Winter's Tale: a Study* (Staples Press, 1947).

maker's Holiday and the Deloney novel on which it is based seem to give a reasonably true picture of the journeyman's fondness for music. And the music while they worked was provided by the workers themselves. If one went to an inn one would be sure to find pipers and fiddlers; and there was dancing in the streets after Evensong on Sundays, in spite of the opposition of the puritans. Morley may not be a reliable witness to the popularity of music, since he was financially interested, but his account of the social embarrassment of the Man Who Could Not Sing is some indication of what was expected of an educated man:[1]

> Supper being ended, and music books according to the custom being brought to the table, the mistress of the house presented me with a part, earnestly requesting me to sing. But when, after many excuses, I protested unfeignedly that I could not, everyone began to wonder. Yea, some whispered to others, demanding how I was brought up.

Between 1588 and 1620 scores of collections of madrigals and airs were published, and some of them went into several editions. They were bought largely by amateurs. From the literary point of view—with which we are concerned—madrigals are not particularly interesting, as the music is so much more important than the words. They consisted often of translations, of previously published verse, of extracts from longer poems, of scraps whose one merit was that they were suitable for singing. A typical example is this tiny poem from Morley's *Canzonets* (1593):

> See, see, mine own sweet jewel,
> What I have for my darling;
> A robin red-breast and a starling.
> These I give both in hope to move thee,
> And yet thou sayst, I do not love thee.

[1] *Plaine and Easie Introduction of Practicall Musicke* (1597). Bruce Pattison, who quotes this passage, shows from a variety of sources that singing was immensely popular.

Another typical example, from Morley's *Madrigals* (1594), was reprinted in *England's Helicon*, though it obviously requires the setting to lift it above triviality:

Hark, jolly shepherd, hark!
  Hark you yond lusty ringing!
How cheerfully the bells dance,
  Whilst the jolly lads are springing.
Go then, why sit we here delaying,
And all yon lads and merry lasses playing?
  How gaily Flora leads it,
  And how she sweetly treads it!
The woods and groves they ring,
  Loudly resounding,
  With echoes sweet rebounding.

The lutanist songs, however, are often excellent lyrics; and the poets, who are mostly anonymous, showed considerable skill in so arranging that the corresponding lines of each stanza, and even individual words, should fit the accompaniment. A few examples may be given. In Jones's *First Book of Airs* (1600) the first lines of the three stanzas of one poem end with the words *grief*, *toil*, and *pain*. Another song in the same collection begins each stanza with corresponding phrases, *For I die . . . But I die . . .* etc. One of Campion's *Airs* (1601) ends the three stanzas respectively with the words "*When flames do die.*" "*When flowers do die.*" "*Thou must die.*" Another Campion poem must be quoted in full:

Author of light, revive my dying spright;
Redeem it from the snares of all-confounding night.
  Lord, light me to thy blessed way:
For blind with worldly vain desires, I wander as a stray.
  Sun and Moon, Stars and underlights I see,
But all their glorious beams are mists and darkness, being compar'd to
    thee.

Fountain of health, my soul's deep wounds recure,
Sweet showers of pity rain, wash my uncleanness pure.
One drop of thy desired grace
The faint and fading heart can raise, and in joy's bosom place.
Sin and Death, Hell and tempting Fiends may rage;
But God his own will guard, and their sharp pains and griefs in time assuage.

It will be apparent, even without the music, how closely the second stanza follows the pattern and colouring of the first. The invocation "Author of light" corresponds to "Fountain of health"; "revive my dying spright" corresponds to "my soul's deep wounds recure"; the redemption motive in line 2 is repeated in "Sweet showers of pity"; "the snares of all-confounding night" may be compared with "wash my uncleanness pure"; "thy blessed way" corresponds to "my desired grace"; in line 5 the list "Sun and Moon, Stars and underlights" corresponds closely in rhythm and emphasis to "Sin and Death, Hell and tempting Fiends"; and in the last line each stanza expresses, in words and music, the triumph of good.[1]

Byrd's first collection of songs appeared in the year of the Armada; others followed in 1589 and 1611. Morley produced nine collections between 1593 and 1601; Dowland four between 1597 and 1612; Jones six between 1600 and 1610; Weelkes five between 1597 and 1608; and there were many others. From the poetic point of view, the most notable collections are those of Campion, some of whose poems were set by Rosseter (1601). Campion's own settings are generally regarded as inferior to his verse; but there are forty or fifty of his poems, very varied in style and subject, which are equal to the best lyrics of the period.

Indeed, in view of the common opinion, it should be stressed that although some themes often recur in the song-

[1] I am indebted to Mr Wilfrid Mellers for calling my attention to this example. Bruce Pattison gives a number of elaborate examples in his book.

ooks, so that complete collections are apt to be tedious, there s amongst the better poets a great variety of treatment. Gaiety and pathos, sin and repentance, sensuous delight in eauty, adoration, wit and humour, bitterness, despair, and oy can all be found there, expressed in an astonishing variety of hythms and stanzas and several different conventions. We are ometimes close to the atmosphere of the sonnet-sequences; ometimes we are in the pastoral world of *England's Helicon*; ometimes in the moral climate of *The Paradise of Dainty Devices*; and sometimes in the fantastic world of nonsense.

Even where the actual subject-matter of the poems is not ery different, the variations on the same theme exemplify he characteristic art of the different poets. Mrs Ing, for example, compares Jonson's "Slow, slow, fresh fount" (No. 129 n this edition) with "Weep you no more, sad fountains" (No. 67) and "Flow not so fast, ye fountains," and she points out he necessity of studying such poems through their versification:

> Their other attributes merely distinguish them as a class from other classes of poetry; their versification gives them existence as individuals within their class.[1]

his may be a slight exaggeration, as the imagery and the hemes are in this case also distinguishable; but the remark ghtly calls attention to the sheer artistry of many Elizabethan ongs. None of the Elizabethans, and least of all Shakespeare, as guilty of warbling his native wood-notes wild.

MISCELLANEOUS

The remaining poems in this collection are taken from colctions of verse by individual poets, and from verse which mained for some years in manuscript. Some great poems ave been omitted because of their familiarity and length (*e.g.*,

[1] Catherine Ing, *Elizabethan Lyrics* (Chatto and Windus, 1951), p. 21.

Spenser's two great odes), though all the great poets are repre
sented. In one other respect the selection gives a false impres
sion of the period, for John Donne was writing many of hi
Songs and Sonnets in the last years of the sixteenth century
and his work was known in manuscript. But a few only of hi
poems are given here, for the somewhat arbitrary reason tha
he could be adequately represented only at the expense o
excluding more characteristically Elizabethan poetry. He se
the tone for a new age, and he is best included in a volume o
metaphysical poetry. Few genuine metaphysical poems go
into the song-books and miscellanies, and Davison, who migh
have included some at least in the second edition of his *Poetic*
Rapsody, apparently preferred other kinds. Yet one of Shakes
peare's sonnets (No. 84 in this edition), and the hauntingl
obscure *Phœnix and the Turtle*, show that it is difficult to dra
the line between the Metaphysicals and their immediate pre
decessors, though Donne probably learnt more from the drama
tists than he did from the lyric writers. Sidney, Ralegh, an
Chapman do, at times, in very different ways, approach th
metaphysical manner. One can find examples of metric
ruggedness (in Wyatt, in the satirists, in Chapman); of avoid
ance of poetic diction (in Greville's Treatises, in Daniel
Epistles, and in many of the later dramatists); of psychologic
realism, of irritation with the Petrarchan convention, and eve
of the dialectical method. Donne, in spite of his great origin
ality, learnt as much from his immediate predecessors as h
rejected. The tendency of modern criticism has been to stre
the resemblances between Elizabethans and Metaphysical
There was no essential difference in their theories; and the
difference of style was largely due to difference of subjec
matter.

The poets of the sixties may safely be ignored in an antholog
of this scope. Googe, Howell, and Turberville are hardly wor
reviving, though a place may be found here for Turberville
version of one of Plato's epigrams:

> My girl, thou gazest much
> Upon the golden skies:
> Would I were Heaven, I would behold
> Thee then with all mine eyes.

n the seventies we get respectable verse from Gascoigne and reton, and *The Shepheards Calender* of Spenser. There were ew volumes of lyrical poetry in the eighties, but in the next wo decades most of the well-known Elizabethans published olumes containing lyrics—Sidney, Spenser, Drayton, Daniel, ir John Davies, Barnfield, Southwell, and many others. The reatest period of the lyric coincided with the finest period of rama, and of narrative verse, with several of the great trans- ations, with the prose of Nashe and Dekker, with Hooker's *aws of Ecclesiastical Polity*, and with Bacon's *Advancement of earning*. In a period which saw the publication of *The Faerie ueene* and the Authorized Version, and witnessed the perform- nces of the plays of Marlowe, Shakespeare, and Jonson, even he greatest lyrics may be regarded as by-products of the nation's oetical energies; yet in no other period of our literature have o many good lyrics been written by so many different poets.

Jonson, in his elegy on Shakespeare, was speaking for his age hen he said that "a good poet's made as well as born." The erfection of the best Elizabethan lyrics was not attained by hance; they were not tossed off in an idle hour by the courtier r statesman, written by hack writers with the printer's devil vaiting for copy, or scribbled down in the Elizabethan under- vorld between one debauch and the next. The teaching of hetoric at school and university, the practice of imitation of he best models, and the popularity of books on rhetoric hroughout the period are indications that the Elizabethan oets, in Yeats's phrase, learnt their trade.

Drayton's first volume, *A Harmony of the Church*, gave no romise that its author would develop into a great poet, and *deas Mirrour* was apparently the work of a poetaster; but by heer hard work, by taking his vocation seriously, Drayton learnt to write well. Many of his greater poems were the fruits of his old age, thirty or forty years after he published his first volume—*The Ballad of Agincourt* (revised for the 1619 volume), *Nimphidia* and *The Shepheards Sirena* (1627), and *The Muses Elizium* (1630). This development can be paralleled in the work of other poets. The sheer artistry of *Epithalamion* is as obvious as its inspiration; and the development of Shakespeare's technique between *Henry VI* and *The Tempest* is as remarkable as the increase in profundity. Even Donne, who may appear to reveal his inmost feelings with the minimum of artistic selection, probably invented and certainly dramatized the poetic situations about which he wrote, and for all his colloquial ease he could not have written as he did without a consummate art.

POEMS FROM MISCELLANIES

I

They flee from me, that sometime did me seek
With naked foot, stalking in my chamber.
I have seen them gentle, tame, and meek,
That now are wild, and do not remember
That sometime they put themselves in danger
To take bread at my hand; and now they range
Busily seeking with a continual change.

Thanked be fortune it hath been otherwise
Twenty times better; but once, in special,
In thin array, after a pleasant guise,
When her loose gown from her shoulders did fall,
And she me caught in her arms long and small,
Therewith all sweetly did me kiss
And softly said, 'Dear heart how like you this?'

It was no dream; I lay broad waking;
But all is turned, thorough my gentleness,
Into a strange fashion of forsaking;
And I have leave to go of her goodness,
And she also to use newfangleness.
But since that I so kindly am served,
I would fain know what she hath deserved.

Sir Thomas Wyatt

2

My lute, awake! perform the last
Labour that thou and I shall waste,
  And end that I have now begun;
For when this song is sung and past,
  My lute, be still, for I have done.

As to be heard where ear is none,
As lead to grave in marble stone,
  My song may pierce her heart as soon.
Should we then sigh, or sing, or moan?
  No, no, my lute, for I have done.

The rocks do not so cruelly
Repulse the waves continually,
  As she my suit and affection;
So that I am past remedy,
  Whereby my lute and I have done.

Proud of the spoil that thou hast got
Of simple hearts thorough love's shot,
  By whom, unkind, thou hast them won,
Think not he hath his bow forgot,
  Although my lute and I have done.

Vengeance shall fall on thy disdain,
That makest but game on earnest pain;
  Think not alone under the sun
Unquit to cause thy lovers plain,
  Although my lute and I have done.

Perchance thee lie withered and old,
The winter nights that are so cold,
  Plaining in vain unto the moon;
Thy wishes then dare not be told.
  Care then who list, for I have done.

And then may chance thee to repent
The time that thou hast lost and spent
  To cause thy lovers sigh and swoon;
Then shalt thou know beauty but lent,
  And wish and want as I have done.

Now cease, my lute! this is the last
Labour that thou and I shall waste,
  And ended is that we begun;
Now is this song both sung and past.
  My lute, be still, for I have done.

Sir Thomas Wyatt

3

O happy dames, that may embrace
  The fruit of your delight,
Help to bewail the woeful case
  And eke the heavy plight
Of me, that wonted to rejoice
The fortune of my pleasant choice;
Good ladies, help to fill my mourning voice.

In ship, freight with remembrance
  Of thoughts and pleasures past,
He sails that hath in governance
  My life while it will last;
With scalding sighs, for lack of gale,
Furthering his hope, that is his sail,
Toward me, the sweet port of his avail.

Alas! how oft in dreams I see
  Those eyes that were my food;
Which sometime so delighted me,
  That yet they do me good;
Wherewith I wake with his return,
Whose absent flame did make me burn:
But when I find the lack, Lord, how I mourn!

When other lovers in arms across
  Rejoice their chief delight,
Drowned in tears, to mourn my loss
  I stand the bitter night
In my window, where I may see
Before the winds how the clouds flee.
Lo! what a mariner love hath made me!

And in green waves when the salt flood
  Doth rise by rage of wind,
A thousand fancies in that mood
  Assail my restless mind.
Alas! now drencheth my sweet foe,
That with the spoil of my heart did go,
And left me; but, alas, why did he so?

And when the seas wax calm again
  To chase fro me annoy,
My doubtful hope doth cause me plain;
  So dread cuts off my joy.
Thus is my wealth mingled with woe,
And of each thought a doubt doth grow;
'Now he comes! Will he come? Alas, no, no!'

Henry Howard, Earl of Surrey

4

Sing lullaby, as women do,
  Wherewith they bring their babes to rest;
And lullaby can I sing too
  As womanly as can the best.
With lullaby they still the child;
And, if I be not much beguil'd,
Full many wanton babes have I,
Which must be still'd with lullaby.

First, lullaby my youthful years,
  It is now time to go to bed;
For crooked age and hoary hairs
  Have won the haven within my head.
With lullaby, then, youth, be still!
With lullaby content thy will!
Since courage quails and comes behind,
Go sleep, and so beguile thy mind!

Next, lullaby my gazing eyes,
  Which wonted were to glance apace;
For every glass may now suffice
  To show the furrows in my face.
With lullaby, then, wink awhile!
With lullaby your looks beguile!
Let no fair face, nor beauty bright,
Entice you eft with vain delight.

And lullaby my wanton will;
  Let reason's rule now reign thy thought,
Since all too late I find by skill
  How dear I have thy fancies bought.
With lullaby now take thine ease!
With lullaby thy doubts appease!
For trust to this, if thou be still,
My body shall obey thy will.

Eke lullaby my loving boy;
  My little Robin, take thy rest!
Since age is cold, and nothing coy,
  Keep close thy coin, for so is best.
With lullaby be thou content!
With lullaby thy lusts relent!
Let others pay which have mo pence,
Thou art too poor for such expense.

Thus, lullaby my youth, mine eyes,
  My will, my ware, and all that was;
I can no mo delays devise,
  But welcome pain, let pleasure pass.
With lullaby now take your leave!
With lullaby your dreams deceive!
And when you rise with waking eye,
Remember then this lullaby!

George Gascoigne

5

When May is in his prime, then may each heart rejoice;
When May bedecks each branch with green, each bird
  strains forth his voice.
The lively sap creeps up into the blooming thorn;
The flowers, which cold in prison kept, now laughs
  the frost to scorn.
All nature's imps triumphs whiles joyful May doth last;
When May is gone, of all the year the pleasant time is past.

May makes the cheerful hue, May breeds and brings new blood;
May marcheth throughout every limb, May makes the merry
  mood.
May pricketh tender hearts their warbling notes to tune;
Full strange it is, yet some we see do make their May in June.
Thus things are strangely wrought whiles joyful May doth last;
Take May in time, when May is gone the pleasant time is past.

All ye that live on earth, and have your May at will,
Rejoice in May, as I do now, and use your May with skill.
Use May while that you may, for May hath but his time,
When all the fruit is gone, it is too late the tree to climb.
Your liking and your lust is fresh whiles May doth last;
When May is gone, of all the year the pleasant time is past.

Richard Edwardes

6

n going to my naked bed as one that would have slept,
heard a wife sing to her child, that long before had wept.
he sighed sore and sang full sweet to bring the babe to rest,
hat would not rest, but cried still, in sucking at her breast.
he was full weary of her watch and grieved with her child,
he rocked it and rated it until on her it smiled.
hen did she say, 'Now have I found the proverb true to prove:
he falling out of faithful friends renewing is of love.'

hen took I paper, pen, and ink, this proverb for to write,
n register for to remain of such a worthy wight.
s she proceeded thus in song unto her little brat,
luch matter uttered she of weight, in place whereas she sat;
nd proved plain there was no beast, nor creature bearing life,
ould well be known to live in love without discord and strife.
hen kissed she her little babe and sware by God above.
The falling out of faithful friends renewing is of love.'

he said that neither king, ne prince, ne lord could live aright,
ntil their puissance they did prove, their manhood, and their
  might;
hen manhood shall be matched so that fear can take no place,
hen weary works makes warriors each other to embrace.
nd leave their force that failed them, which did consume the
  rout,
hat might by force with love have liv'd the term of nature out.
hen did she sing as one that thought no man could her
  reprove,
he falling out of faithful friends renewing is of love.'

e said she saw no fish, ne fowl, nor beast within her haunt
hat met a stranger in their kind, but could give it a taunt.
nce flesh might not endure, but rest must wrath succeed,
nd force the fight to fall to play in pasture where they feed,

So noble Nature can well end the works she hath begun,
And bridle well that will not cease her tragedy in some.
Thus in her song she oft rehears'd, as did her well behove,
'The falling out of faithful friends renewing is of love.'

'I marvel much, perdy!' (quoth she), 'for to behold the rout,
To see man, woman, boy, and beast, to toss the world about.
Some kneel, some crouch, some beck, some check, and som
can smoothly smile,
And some embrace others in arms, and there think many a wile
Some stand aloof at cap and knee, some humble and some stout
Yet are they never friends indeed until they once fall out.'
Thus ended she her song, and said, before she did remove,
'The falling out of faithful friends renewing is of love.'

Richard Edwardes

7

If thou in surety safe wilt sit,
If thou delight at rest to dwell,
Spend no more words than shall seem fit,
Let tongue in silence talk expel:
In all things that thou seest men bent,
See all! say nought! hold thee content!

In worldly works degrees are three,
Makers, doers, and lookers-on:
The lookers-on have liberty
Both the others to judge upon:
Wherefore, in all, as men are bent,
See all! say nought! hold thee content!

The makers oft are in fault found;
The doers doubt of praise or shame;
The lookers-on find surest ground,
They have the fruit, yet free from blame:
This doth persuade in all here meant,
See all! say nought! hold thee content!

The proverb is not south and west,
  Which hath been said long time ago,
"Of little meddling cometh rest,
  The busy man never wanteth woe":
The best way is, in all worlds sent,
See all! say nought! hold thee content!

Jasper Heywood

8

Ay me, ay me! I sigh to see the scythe afield;
  Down goeth the grass, soon wrought to wither'd hay.
Ay me, alas! ay me, alas! that beauty needs must yield,
  And princes pass, as grass doth fade away.

Ay me, ay me! that life cannot have lasting leave,
  Nor gold take hold of everlasting joy.
Ay me, alas! ay me, alas! that time hath talents to receive,
  And yet no time can make a sure stay.

Ay me, ay me! that wit cannot have wished choice,
  Nor wish can win that will desires to see.
Ay me, alas! ay me, alas! that mirth can promise no rejoice,
  Nor study tell what afterward shall be.

Ay me, ay me! that no sure staff is given to age,
  Nor age can give sure wit that youth will take.
Ay me, alas! ay me, alas! that no counsel wise and sage
  Will shun the show that all doth mar and make.

Ay me, ay me! come Time, shear on and shake thy hay;
  It is no boot to balk thy bitter blows.
Ay me, alas! ay me, alas! come Time, take every thing away,
  For all is thine, be it good or bad that grows.

Thomas Proctor (?)

9

A nosegay, lacking flowers fresh,
To you now I do send;
Desiring you to look thereon,
When that you may intend:
For flowers fresh begin to fade,
And Boreas in the field,
Even with his hard congealed frost
No better flowers doth yield.

But if that winter could have sprung
A sweeter flower than this,
I would have sent it presently
To you withouten miss.
Accept this then as time doth serve,
Be thankful for the same;
Despite it not, but keep it well,
And mark each flower his name.

Lavender is for lovers true,
Which evermore be fain,
Desiring always for to have
Some pleasure for their pain:
And when that they obtained have
The love that they require,
Then have they all their perfect joy,
And quenched is the fire.

Rosemary is for remembrance
Between us day and night;
Wishing that I might always have
You present in my sight.
And when I cannot have,
As I have said before,
Then Cupid with his deadly dart
Doth wound my heart full sore

Sage is for sustenance
  That should man's life sustain;
For I do still lie languishing
  Continually in pain,
And shall do still until I die
  Except thou favour show:
My pain and all my grievous smart
  Full well you do it know.

Fennel is for flatterers,
  An evil thing it is sure,
But I have always meant truly,
  With constant heart most pure;
And will continue in the same
  As long as life doth last,
Still hoping for a joyful day
  When all our pains be past.

Violet is for faithfulness,
  Which in me shall abide;
Hoping likewise that from your heart
  You will not let it slide:
And will continue in the same
  As you have now begun;
And then for ever to abide;
  Then you my heart have won.

Thyme is to try me,
  As each be tried must,
Letting you know while life doth last
  I will not be unjust;
And if I should, I would to God
  To hell my soul should bear,
And eke also that Belzebub
  With teeth he should me tear.

Roses is to rule me
  With reason as you will,
For to be still obedient,
  Your mind for to fulfil;
And thereto will not disagree
  In nothing that you say,
But will content your mind truly
  In all things that I may.

Gillyflowers is for gentleness,
  Which in me shall remain,
Hoping that no sedition shall
  Depart our hearts in twain.
As soon the sun shall lose his course,
  The moon against her kind
Shall have no light, if that I do
  Once put you from my mind.

Carnations is for graciousness,
  Mark that now by the way,
Have no regard to flatterers,
  Nor pass not what they say.
For they will come with lying tales,
  Your ears for to fulfil:
In any case do not consent
  Nothing unto their will.

Marigolds is for marriage,
  That would our minds suffice,
Lest that suspicion of us twain
  By any means should rise:
As for my part, I do not care,
  Myself I will still use,
That all the women in the world
  For you I will refuse.

Pennyroyal is to print your love
So deep within my heart,
That when you look this nosegay on,
My pain you may impart;
And when that you have read the same,
Consider well my woe,
Think ye then how to recompense
Even him that loves you so.

Cowslips is for counsel,
For secrets us between,
That none but you and I alone
Should know the thing we mean:
And if you will thus wisely do,
As I think to be best,
Then have you surely won the field
And set my heart at rest.

I pray you keep this nosegay well,
And set by it some store:
And thus farewell! the gods thee guide
Both now and evermore!
Not as the common sort do use,
To set it in your breast,
That when the smell is gone away,
On ground he takes his rest.

William Hunnis (?)

10

When wert thou born, Desire?
In pride and pomp of May.
By whom, sweet boy, wert thou begot?
By Self Conceit, men say.
Tell me, who was thy nurse?
Fresh Youth, in sugar'd joy.

What was thy meat and daily food?
  Sad sighs and great annoy.
What haddest thou to drink?
  Unfeigned lovers' tears.
What cradle wert thou rocked in?
  In hope devoid of fears.
What brought thee to thy sleep?
  Sweet thoughts, which liked me best.
And where is now thy dwelling-place?
  In gentle hearts I rest.
Doth company displease?
  It doth, in many one.
Where would Desire then choose to be?
  He loves to muse alone.
What feedeth most thy sight?
  To gaze on favour still.
Whom find'st thou most thy foe?
  Disdain of my good will.
Will ever age or death
  Bring thee unto decay?
No, no! Desire both lives and dies
  A thousand times a day.

Edward de Vere, Earl of Oxford

II

O night, O jealous night, repugnant to my pleasures,
  O night so long desir'd, yet cross to my content,
There's none but only thou that can perform my pleasures,
  Yet none but only thou that hindereth my intent.

Thy beams, thy spiteful beams, thy lamps that burn too brightly
  Discover all my trains, and naked lay my drifts;
That night by night I hope, yet fail my purpose nightly,
  Thy envious glaring gleam defeateth so my shifts.

weet night, withhold thy beams, withhold them till to-morrow,
Whose joys, in lack so long, a hell of torments breeds;
weet night, sweet gentle night, do not prolong my sorrow,
Desire is guide to me, and love no lodestar needs.

et sailors gaze on stars and moon so freshly shining,
Let them that miss the way be guided by the light;
know my lady's bower, there needs no more divining;
Affection sees in dark, and love hath eyes by night.

ame Cynthia, couch awhile, hold in thy horns for shining,
And glad not louring night with thy too glorious rays:
ut be she dim and dark, tempestuous and repining.
That in her spite my sport may work thy endless praise.

nd when my will is wrought, then, Cynthia, shine, good lady,
All other nights and days in honour of that night,
hat happy, heavenly night, that night so dark and shady,
Wherein my love had eyes that lighted my delight.

Anonymous

12

Now what is Love? I pray thee, tell.
It is that fountain and that well,
Where pleasure and repentance dwell.
It is perhaps that sauncing bell,
That tolls all in to heaven or hell:
And this is love, as I hear tell.

Yet what is love? I pray thee say.
It is a work on holy-day;
It is December match'd with May;
When lusty bloods, in fresh array,
Hear ten months after of the play;
And this is love, as I hear say,

Yet what is love? I pray thee sayn.
It is a sunshine mix'd with rain;
It is a tooth-ache, or like pain;
It is a game where none doth gain;
The lass saith no, and would full fain;
And this is love, as I hear sayn.

Yet what is love? I pray thee say.
It is a yea, it is a nay,
A pretty kind of sporting fray;
It is a thing will soon away;
Then take the vantage while you may:
And this is love, as I hear say.

Yet what is love? I pray thee show.
A thing that creeps, it cannot go;
A prize that passeth to and fro;
A thing for one, a thing for mo;
And he that proves must find it so:
And this is love, sweet friend, I trow.

Sir Walter Ralegh (

13

Sought by the world, and hath the world disdained,
Is she, my heart, for whom thou dost endure;
Unto whose grace sith kings have not obtained,
Sweet is thy choice, though loss of life be sour;
Yet to the man, whose youth such pains must prove,
No better end than that which comes by love.

Steer then thy course unto the port of death,
(Sith thy hard hap no better hap may find,)
Where, when thou shalt unlade thy latest breath,
Envy herself shall swim, to save thy mind;
Whose body sunk in search to gain that shore
Where many a prince had perished before.

And yet, my heart, it might have been foreseen,
  Sith skilful medicines mend each kind of grief;
Then in my breast full safely hadst thou been.
  But thou, my heart, wouldst never me believe,
    Who told thee true when first thou didst aspire,
    Death was the end of every such desire.

Anonymous

14

Sweet violets, Love's paradise, that spread
  Your gracious odours, which you couched bear
    Within your paly faces,
Upon the gentle wing of some calm breathing wind
  That plays amidst the plain,
  If by the favour of propitious stars you gain
Such grace as in my lady's bosom place to find,
    Be proud to touch those places;
  And when her warmth your moisture forth doth wear,
Whereby her dainty parts are sweetly fed,
  Your honours of the flowery meads, I pray,
You pretty daughters of the earth and sun,
  With mild and seemly breathing straight display
My bitter sighs that have my heart undone.

Vermilion roses, that with new day's rise
  Display your crimson folds, fresh-looking, fair,
    Whose radiant bright disgraces
The rich adorned rays of roseate rising morn,
  Ah! if her virgin's hand
  Do pluck your pure, ere Phoebus view the land
And vail your gracious pomp in lovely nature's scorn,
    If chance my mistress traces
  Fast by your flowers to take the summer's air,
Then, woeful blushing, tempt her glorious eyes
  To spread their tears, Adonis' death reporting,

And tell Love's torments, sorrowing for her friend,
Whose drops of blood within your leaves consorting,
Report fair Venus' moans withouten end.
Then may remorse, in pitying of my smart,
Dry up my tears, and dwell within her heart.

Anonymous

15

Come, little babe, come silly soul,
Thy father's shame, thy mother's grief,
Born as I doubt to all our dole,
And to thyself unhappy chief:
Sing lullaby and lap it warm,
Poor soul that thinks no creature harm.

Thou little think'st and less dost know
The cause of this thy mother's moan;
Thou want'st the wit to wail her woe,
And I myself am all alone;
Why dost thou weep? why dost thou wail,
And knowest not yet what thou dost ail?

Come, little wretch! Ah, silly heart!
Mine only joy, what can I more?
If there be any wrong thy smart,
That may the destinies implore,
'Twas I, I say, against my will:
I wail the time, but be thou still.

And dost thou smile? O! thy sweet face!
Would God himself he might thee see!
No doubt thou wouldst soon purchase grace,
I know right well, for thee and me:
But come to mother, babe, and play,
For father false is fled away.

Sweet boy, if it by fortune chance
Thy father home again to send,
If death do strike me with his lance,
Yet may'st thou me to him commend:
If any ask thy mother's name,
Tell how by love she purchas'd blame.

Then will his gentle heart soon yield:
I know him of a noble mind;
Although a lion in the field,
A lamb in town thou shalt him find.
Ask blessing, babe, be not afraid!
His sugar'd words hath me betray'd.

Then may'st thou joy and be right glad,
Although in woe I seem to moan.
Thy father is no rascal lad,
A noble youth of blood and bone;
His glancing looks, if he once smile,
Right honest women may beguile.

Come, little boy, and rock asleep!
Sing lullaby, and be thou still!
I, that can do nought else but weep,
Will sit by thee and wail my fill:
God bless my babe, and lullaby,
From this thy father's quality.

Nicholas Breton

16

Crabbed age and youth cannot live together:
Youth is full of pleasance, age is full of care;
Youth like summer morn, age like winter weather;
Youth like summer brave, age like winter bare.

Youth is full of sport, age's breath is short;
  Youth is nimble, age is lame;
Youth is hot and bold, age is weak and cold;
  Youth is wild, and age is tame.
Age, I do abhor thee, youth I do adore thee;
  O! my love, my love is young:
Age, I do defy thee. O! sweet shepherd, hie thee,
  For methinks thou stays too long.

William Shakespeare (?)

17

As withereth the primrose by the river,
  As fadeth summer's sun from gliding fountains,
As vanisheth the light-blown bubble ever,
  As melteth snow upon the mossy mountains:
So melts, so vanisheth, so fades, so withers
  The rose, the shine, the bubble, and the snow
Of praise, pomp, glory, joy (which short life gathers),
  Fair praise, vain pomp, sweet glory, brittle joy.
The wither'd primrose by the mourning river,
  The faded summer's sun from weeping fountains,
The light-blown bubble vanished for ever,
  The molten snow upon the naked mountains,
Are emblems that the treasures we up-lay
Soon wither, vanish, fade, and melt away.

For as the snow, whose lawn did overspread
  Th' ambitious hills, which giant-like did threat
To pierce the heaven with their aspiring head,
  Naked and bare doth leave their scraggy seat;
Whenas the bubble, which did empty fly
  The dalliance of the undiscerned wind,
On whose calm rolling waves it did rely,
  Hath shipwreck made, where it did dalliance find;

\nd when the sunshine which dissolv'd the snow,
Colour'd the bubble with a pleasant vary,
\nd made the rathe and timely primrose grow,
Swarth clouds withdraw, which longer time do tarry:
)! what is praise, pomp, glory, joy, but so
\s shine by fountains, bubbles, flowers, or snow?

Edmund Bolton

18

Gorbo, as thou cam'st this way
By yonder little hill,
Or as thou through the fields didst stray,
Saw'st thou my Daffodil?

She's in a frock of Lincoln green,
Which colour likes her sight,
And never hath her beauty seen
But through a veil of white;

Than roses, richer to behold,
That trim up lovers' bowers,
The pansy and the marigold,
Though Phoebus' paramours.

"Thou well describ'st the daffodil;
It is not full an hour
Since by the spring near younder hill
I saw that lovely flower."

Yet my fair flower thou didst not meet,
Nor news of her didst bring,
And yet my Daffodil's more sweet
Than that by yonder spring.

"I saw a shepherd that doth keep
In yonder field of lilies,
Was making, as he fed his sheep,
A wreath of daffodillies."

Yet, Gorbo, thou delud'st me still,
My flower thou didst not see;
For know, my pretty Daffodil
Is worn of none but me.

To show itself but near her seat
No lily is so bold,
Except to shade her from the heat,
Or keep her from the cold.

"Through yonder dale as I did pass,
Descending from the hill,
I met a smirking bonny lass;
They call her Daffodil;

"Whose presence, as along she went,
The pretty flowers did greet
As though their heads they downward bent
With homage to her feet;

"And all the shepherds that were nigh,
From top of every hill
Unto the valleys, loud did cry,
'There goes sweet Daffodil!'"

Ay, gentle shepherd, now with joy
Thou all my flocks dost fill,
That's she alone, kind shepherd's boy;
Let us to Daffodil.

Michael Drayton

19

In the merry month of May,
In a morn by break of day,
Forth I walk'd by the wood side,
Whereas May was in her pride.
There I spied all alone
Phyllida and Corydon.
Much ado there was, God wot,
He would love and she would not.
She said, never man was true;
He said, none was false to you.
He said, he had lov'd her long;
She said, love should have no wrong.
Corydon would kiss her then;
She said, maids must kiss no men,
Till they did for good and all.
Then she made the shepherd call
All the heavens to witness truth,
Never lov'd a truer youth.
Thus with many a pretty oath,
Yea and nay, and faith and troth,
Such as silly shepherds use,
When they will not love abuse,
Love which had been long deluded,
Was with kisses sweet concluded:
And Phyllida with garlands gay
Was made the Lady of the May.

Nicholas Breton

20

Jolly shepherd, shepherd on a hill,
On a hill so merrily,
On a hill so cheerily,
Fear not, shepherd, there to pipe thy fill;
Fill every dale, fill every plain:
Both sing and say, "Love feels no pain."

Jolly shepherd, shepherd on a green,
On a green so merrily,
On a green so cheerily,
Be thy voice shrill, be thy mirth seen,
Heard to each swain, seen to each trull:
Both sing and say, "Love's joy is full."

Jolly shepherd, shepherd in the sun,
In the sun so merrily,
In the sun so cheerily,
Sing forth thy songs, and let thy rhymes run
Down to the dales, to the hills above:
Both sing and say, "No life to love."

Jolly shepherd, shepherd in the shade,
In the shade so merrily,
In the shade so cheerily,
Joy in thy life, life of shepherd's trade,
Joy in thy love, love full of glee:
Both sing and say, "Sweet love for me."

Jolly shepherd, shepherd here or there,
Here or there so merrily,
Here or there so cheerily,
Or in thy chat, either at thy cheer,
In every jig, in every lay:
Both sing and say, "Love lasts for aye."

Jolly shepherd, shepherd Daphnis' love,
Daphnis' love so merrily,
Daphnis' love so cheerily,
Let thy fancy never more remove,
Fancy be fix'd, fix'd not to fleet:
Still sing and say, "Love's yoke is sweet."

John Wotton

21

PHYLLIDA: Corydon, arise, my Corydon!
Titan shineth clear.
CORYDON: Who is it that calleth Corydon?
Who is it that I hear?
PHYLLIDA: Phyllida, thy true Love, calleth thee,
Arise then, arise then,
Arise and keep thy flock with me!
CORYDON: Phyllida, my true Love, is it she?
I come then, I come then,
I come and keep my flock with thee.

PHYLLIDA: Here are cherries ripe, my Corydon;
Eat them for my sake.
CORYDON: Here's my oaten pipe, my lovely one,
Sport for thee to make.
PHYLLIDA: Here are threads, my true Love, fine as silk,
To knit thee, to knit thee
A pair of stockings white as milk.
CORYDON: Here are reeds, my true Love, fine and neat,
To make thee, to make thee
A bonnet to withstand the heat.

PHYLLIDA: I will gather flowers, my Corydon,
To set in thy cap.
CORYDON: I will gather pears, my lovely one,
To put in thy lap.
PHYLLIDA: I will buy my true Love garters gay
For Sundays, for Sundays,
To wear about his legs so tall.
CORYDON: I will buy my true Love yellow say
For Sundays, for Sundays,
To wear about her middle small.

PHYLLIDA: When my Corydon sits on a hill
Making melody—
CORYDON: When my lovely one goes to her wheel
Singing cheerily—
PHYLLIDA: Sure methinks my true Love doth excel
For sweetness, for sweetness,
Sir Pan, that old Arcadian knight.
CORYDON: And methinks my true Love bears the bell
For clearness, for clearness,
Beyond the nymphs that be so bright.

PHYLLIDA: Had my Corydon, my Corydon,
Been, alack! her swain—
CORYDON: Had my lovely one, my lovely one,
Been in Ida plain—
PHYLLIDA: Cynthia Endymion had refused,
Preferring, preferring,
My Corydon to play withal.
CORYDON: The queen of love had been excused,
Bequeathing, bequeathing,
My Phyllida the golden ball.

PHYLLIDA: Yonder comes my mother, Corydon.
Whither shall I fly?
CORYDON: Under yonder beech, my lovely one,
While she passeth by.
PHYLLIDA: Say to her thy true Love was not here;
Remember, remember,
To-morrow is another day.
CORYDON: Doubt me not, my true Love, do not fear;
Farewell then, farewell then,
Heaven keep our loves alway.

Anonymous

22

Diaphenia, like the daffodowndilly,
White as the sun, fair as the lily,
Heigh ho, how I do love thee!
I do love thee as my lambs
Are beloved of their dams;
How blest were I if thou wouldst prove me!

Diaphenia, like the spreading roses,
That in thy sweets all sweets encloses,
Fair sweet, how I do love thee!
I do love thee as each flower
Loves the sun's life-giving power,
For, dead, thy breath to life might move me.

Diaphenia, like to all things blessed,
When all thy praises are expressed,
Dear joy, how I do love thee!
As the birds do love the spring,
Or the bees their careful king:
Then in requite, sweet virgin, love me!

Henry Chettle

23

Come live with me and be my love,
And we will all the pleasures prove,
That hills and valleys, dales and fields,
And all the craggy mountains yields.

There we will sit upon the rocks,
And see the shepherds feed their flocks,
By shallow rivers to whose falls
Melodious birds sing madrigals.

And I will make thee beds of roses
With a thousand fragrant posies,
A cap of flowers, and a kirtle
Embroider'd all with leaves of myrtle;

A gown made of the finest wool
Which from our pretty lambs we pull;
Fair lined slippers for the cold;
With buckles of the purest gold;

A belt of straw and ivy buds,
With coral clasps and amber studs:
And if these pleasures may thee move,
Come live with me and be my love.

The shepherd-swains shall dance and sing
For thy delight each May morning:
If these delights thy mind may move,
Then live with me and be my love.

Christopher Marlowe

24

If all the world and love were young,
And truth in every shepherd's tongue,
These pretty pleasures might we move
To live with thee and be thy love.

Time drives the flocks from field to fold,
When rivers rage and rocks grow cold,
And Philomel becometh dumb;
The rest complain of cares to come.

The flowers do fade, and wanton fields
To wayward winter reckoning yields;
A honey tongue, a heart of gall,
Is fancy's spring, but sorrow's fall.

Thy gowns, thy shoes, thy beds of roses,
Thy cap, thy kirtle, and thy posies
Soon break, soon wither, soon forgotten,
In folly ripe, in reason rotten.

Thy belt of straw and ivy buds,
Thy coral clasps and amber studs,
All these in me no means can move
To come to thee and be thy love.

But could youth last and love still breed,
Had joys no date no age no need,
Then these delights my mind might move
To live with thee and be thy love.

Sir Walter Ralegh

25

Sweet, if you like and love me still,
And yield me love for my goodwill,
And do not from your promise start,
When your fair hand gave me your heart;
If dear to you I be,
As you are dear to me;
Then yours I am, and will be ever,
Nor time nor place my love shall sever,
But faithful will I still persever,
Like constant marble stone,
Loving but you alone.

But if you favour mo than me,
Who love thee still, and none but thee;
If others do the harvest gain
That's due to me for all my pain;
If that you love to range,
And oft to chop and change:

Then get you some new-fangled mate;
My doting love shall turn to hate,
Esteeming you, though too too late,
Not worth a pebble stone,
Loving not me alone.

Francis Davin

26

At her fair hands how have I grace entreated,
With prayers oft repeated,
Yet still my love is thwarted:
Heart, let her go, for she'll not be converted.
Say, shall she go?
O! no, no, no, no, no.
She is most fair, though she be marble-hearted.

How often have my sighs declared mine anguish,
Wherein I daily languish,
Yet doth she still procure it:
Heart, let her go, for I cannot endure it.
Say, shall she go?
O! no, no, no, no, no.
She gave the wound, and she alone must cure it.

The trickling tears, that down my cheeks have flowed
My love have often showed;
Yet still unkind I prove her:
Heart, let her go, for nought I do can move her.
Say, shall she go?
O! no, no, no, no, no.
Though me she hate, I cannot choose but love her.

But shall I still a true affection owe her,
Which prayers, sighs, tears do shew her;
And shall she still disdain me?

Heart, let her go, if they no grace can gain me.
Say, shall she go?
O! no, no, no, no, no.
She made me hers, and hers she will retain me.

But if the love that hath, and still doth burn me,
No love at length return me,
Out of my thoughts I'll set her:
Heart, let her go, oh heart, I pray thee let her.
Say, shall she go?
O! no, no, no, no, no.
Fix'd in the heart, how can the heart forget her?

But if I weep and sigh, and often wail me,
Till tears, sighs, prayers fail me,
Shall yet my love persever?
Heart, let her go, if she will right thee never.
Say, shall she go?
O! no, no, no, no, no.
Tears, sighs, prayers fail, but true love lasteth ever.

Walter Davison

27

Sweet Love, mine only treasure,
For service long unfeigned,
Wherein I nought have gained,
Vouchsafe this little pleasure,
To tell me in what part
My lady keeps my heart.

If in her hair so slender,
Like golden nets untwined,
Which fire and art have fined,
Her thrall my heart I render,
For ever to abide
With locks so dainty tied.

If in her eyes she bind it,
  Wherein that fire was framed,
  By which it is inflamed,
I dare not look to find it;
  I only wish it sight,
  To see that pleasant light.

But if her breast have deigned
  With kindness to receive it,
  I am content to leave it,
Though death thereby were gained;
  Then, lady, take your own,
  That lives for you alone.

A. W.

28

The night, say all, was made for rest;
  And so say I, but not for all:
To them the darkest nights are best,
  Which give them leave asleep to fall;
    But I that seek my rest by light
    Hate sleep, and praise the clearest night.

Bright was the moon, as bright as day,
  And Venus glister'd in the west,
Whose light did lead the ready way,
  That brought me to my wished rest:
    Then each of them increas'd their light
    While I enjoy'd her heavenly sight.

Say, gentle dames, what mov'd your mind
  To shine so bright above your wont?
Would Phoebe fair Endymion find?
  Would Venus see Adonis hunt?
    No, no, you feared by her sight
    To lose the praise of beauty bright.

At last for shame you shrunk away,
And thought to reave the world of light;
Then shone my dame with brighter ray,
Than that which comes from Phoebus' sight:
None other light but hers I praise,
Whose nights are clearer than the days.

A. W

29

Bright shines the sun; play, beggars, play!
Here's scraps enough to serve to-day.

What noise of viols is so sweet
As when our merry clappers ring?
What mirth doth want where beggars meet?
A beggar's life is for a king.
Eat, drink, and play; sleep when we list;
Go where we will, so stocks be miss'd.
Bright shines the sun; play, beggars, play!
Here's scraps enough to serve to-day.

The world is ours, and ours alone;
For we alone have worlds at will;
We purchase not, all is our own;
Both fields and streets we beggars fill.
Nor care to get, nor fear to keep,
Did ever break a beggar's sleep.
Bright shines the sun; play, beggars, play!
Here's scraps enough to serve to-day.

A hundred head of black and white
Upon our gowns securely feed;
If any dare his master bite,
He dies therefore, as sure as creed.
Thus beggars lord it as they please,
And none but beggars live at ease.
Bright shines the sun; play, beggars, play!
Here's scraps enough to serve to-day.

A. W.

30

My love in her attire doth show her wit,
It doth so well become her:
For every season she hath dressings fit,
For winter, spring, and summer.
No beauty she doth miss,
When all her robes are on:
But Beauty's self she is,
When all her robes are gone.

Anonymous

31

Absence, hear thou my protestation
Against thy strength,
Distance, and length:
Do what thou canst for alteration,
For hearts of truest mettle
Absence doth join, and time doth settle.

Who loves a mistress of such quality,
He soon hath found
Affection's ground
Beyond time, place, and all mortality.
To hearts that cannot vary
Absence is present, time doth tarry.

My senses want their outward motions
Which now within
Reason doth win,
Redoubled in her secret notions:
Like rich men that take pleasure
In hiding, more than handling treasure.

By absence this good means I gain,
That I can catch her
Where none can watch her,
In some close corner of my brain:
There I embrace and kiss her,
And so I both enjoy and miss her.

John Hoskins (?)

32

Go, soul, the body's guest,
Upon a thankless arrant;
Fear not to touch the best;
The truth shall be thy warrant.
Go, since I needs must die,
And give the world the lie.

Say to the court, it glows
And shines like rotten wood;
Say to the church, it shows
What's good, and doth no good:
If church and court reply,
Then give them both the lie.

Tell potentates, they live
Acting by other's action,
Not loved unless they give,
Not strong but by affection:
If potentates reply,
Give potentates the lie.

Tell men of high condition
That manage the estate,
Their purpose is ambition,
Their practice only hate:
And if they once reply,
Then give them all the lie.

Tell them that brave it most,
  They beg for more by spending,
Who, in their greatest cost,
  Seek nothing but commending:
    And if they make reply,
    Then give them all the lie.

Tell zeal it wants devotion;
  Tell love it is but lust;
Tell time it metes but motion;
  Tell flesh it is but dust:
    And wish them not reply,
    For thou must give the lie.

Tell age it daily wasteth;
  Tell honour how it alters;
Tell beauty how she blasteth;
  Tell favour how it falters:
    And as they shall reply,
    Give every one the lie.

Tell wit how much it wrangles
  In tickle points of niceness;
Tell wisdom she entangles
  Herself in over-wiseness:
    And when they do reply,
    Straight give them both the lie.

Tell physic of her boldness;
  Tell skill it is prevention;
Tell charity of coldness;
  Tell law it is contention:
    And as they do reply,
    So give them still the lie.

Tell fortune of her blindness;
  Tell nature of decay;
Tell friendship of unkindness;
  Tell justice of delay:
    And if they will reply,
    Then give them all the lie.

Tell arts they have no soundness
  But vary by esteeming;
Tell schools they want profoundness,
  And stand too much on seeming:
    If arts and schools reply,
    Give arts and schools the lie.

Tell faith it's fled the city;
  Tell how the country erreth;
Tell, manhood shakes off pity;
  Tell, virtue least preferreth:
    And if they do reply,
    Spare not to give the lie.

So when thou hast, as I
  Commanded thee, done blabbing,
Although to give the lie
  Deserves no less than stabbing,
    Stab at thee he that will,
    No stab thy soul can kill.

Sir Walter Ralegh

SONNETS

33

You that in love find luck and abundance,
And live in lust and joyful jollity,
Arise, for shame, do away your sluggardy!
Arise, I say, do May some observance!
Let me in bed lie dreaming in mischance;
Let me remember the haps most unhappy,
That me betide in May most commonly,
As one whom love list little to advance.
Sepham said true that my nativity
Mischanced was with the ruler of the May;
He guess'd, I prove, of that the verity;
In May my wealth, and eke my life I say
Have stonde so oft in such perplexity.
Rejoice! let me dream of your felicity.

Sir Thomas Wyatt

34

The pillar perish'd is whereto I lent,
The strongest stay of mine unquiet mind;
The like of it no man again can find,
From East to West still seeking though he went.
To mine unhappe! for hap away hath rent
Of all my joy the very bark and rind;
And I, alas, by chance am thus assign'd
Dearly to mourn till death do it relent.
But since that thus it is by destiny,
What can I more but have a woeful heart,
My pen in plaint, my voice in careful cry,

My mind in woe, my body full of smart,
  And I myself my self always to hate,
  Till dreadful death do ease my doleful state?

Sir Thomas Wyatt

35

The soote season, that bud and bloom forth brings,
  With green hath clad the hill and eke the vale.
The nightingale with feathers new she sings;
  The turtle to her make hath told her tale.
Summer is come, for every spray now springs.
  The hart hath hung his old head on the pale;
The buck in brake his winter coat he flings;
  The fishes float with new repaired scale;
The adder all her slough away she slings;
  The swift swallow pursueth the flies smale;
The busy bee her honey now she mings;
  Winter is worn that was the flowers' bale.
And thus I see among these pleasant things
Each care decays; and yet my sorrow springs.

Henry Howard, Earl of Surrey

36

Alas! so all things now do hold their peace,
  Heaven and earth disturbed in no thing.
The beasts, the air, the birds their song do cease;
  The nightes chare the stars about doth bring;
Calm is the sea; the waves work less and less.
  So am not I, whom love, alas! doth wring,
Bringing before my face the great increase
  Of my desires, whereat I weep and sing,
In joy and woe, as in a doubtful ease:
  For my sweet thoughts sometime do pleasure bring;
But by and by, the cause of my disease
  Gives me a pang, that inwardly doth sting,

When that I think what grief it is again,
To live and lack the thing should rid my pain.

Henry Howard, Earl of Surrey

37

Your words, my friend, right healthful caustics, blame
My young mind marr'd, whom Love doth windlass so;
That mine own writings like bad servants show
My wits, quick in vain thoughts, in virtue lame;
That Plato I read for nought, but if he tame
Such coltish years; that to my birth I owe
Nobler desires, lest else that friendly foe,
Great Expectation, wear a train of shame.
But since mad March great promise made of me,
If now the May of my years much decline,
What can be hop'd my harvest-time will be?
Sure you say well, your wisdom's golden mine
Dig deep with learning's spade. Now tell me this:
Hath this world ought so fair as Stella is?

Sir Philip Sidney

38

With how sad steps, O Moon, thou climb'st the skies!
How silently, and with how wan a facc!
What! may it be that even in heavenly placc
That busy archer his sharp arrows tries?
Sure, if that long-with-love-acquainted eyes
Can judge of love, thou feel'st a lover's case;
I read it in thy looks; thy languish'd grace
To me, that feel the like, thy state descries.
Then, even of fellowship, O Moon, tell me,
Is constant love deem'd there but want of wit?
Are beauties there as proud as here they be?
Do they above love to be loved, and yet
Those lovers scorn whom that love doth possess?
Do they call virtue there ungratefulness?

Sir Philip Sidney

39

I might—unhappy word!—oh me, I might,
  And then would not, or could not, see my bliss;
Till now, wrapp'd in a most infernal night,
  I find how heavenly day, wretch, I did miss;
Heart, rent thyself, thou dost thyself but right;
  No lovely Paris made thy Helen his,
No force, no fraud, robb'd thee of thy delight,
  Nor Fortune of thy fortune author is;
But to myself myself did give the blow,
  While too much wit, forsooth, so troubled me
That I respects for both our sakes must show,
  And yet could not by rising morn foresee
    How fair a day was near; oh, punished eyes,
    That I had been more foolish, or more wise!

Sir Philip Sidney

40

Come, Sleep, O Sleep, the certain knot of peace,
  The baiting place of wit, the balm of woe,
The poor man's wealth, the prisoner's release,
  Th' indifferent judge between the high and low;
With shield of proof shield me from out the prease
  Of those fierce darts despair at me doth throw;
O make in me those civil wars to cease;
  I will good tribute pay, if thou do so.
Take thou of me smooth pillows, sweetest bed,
  A chamber deaf to noise, and blind to light,
A rosy garland and a weary head;
  And if these things, as being thine by right,
    Move not thy heavy grace, thou shalt in me,
    Livelier than elsewhere, Stella's image see.

Sir Philip Sidney

41

Highway, since you my chief Parnassus be,
And that my Muse, to some ears not unsweet,
Tempers her words to trampling horses' feet
More oft than to a chamber-melody,
Now, blessed you, bear onward blessed me
To her, where I my heart, safe-left, shall meet;
My Muse and I must you of duty greet
With thanks and wishes, wishing thankfully.
Be you still fair, honour'd by public heed;
By no encroachment wrong'd, nor time forgot;
Nor blam'd for blood, nor sham'd for sinful deed;
And, that you know I envy you no lot
Of highest wish, I wish you so much bliss,
Hundreds of years you Stella's feet may kiss!

Sir Philip Sidney

42

Thou blind man's mark, thou fool's self-chosen snare,
Fond fancy's scum, and dregs of scatter'd thought;
Band of all evils, cradle of causeless care;
Thou web of will, whose end is never wrought;
Desire, desire! I have too dearly bought,
With price of mangled mind, thy worthless ware;
Too long, too long, asleep thou hast me brought,
Who should my mind to higher things prepare,
But yet in vain thou hast my ruin sought;
In vain thou madest me to vain things aspire;
In vain thou kindlest all thy smoky fire;
For virtue hath this better lesson taught,
Within myself to seek my only hire,
Desiring nought but how to kill desire.

Sir Philip Sidney

43

Leave me, O Love, which reachest but to dust;
  And thou, my mind, aspire to higher things;
Grow rich in that which never taketh rust;
  Whatever fades but fading pleasure brings.
Draw in thy beams, and humble all thy might
  To that sweet yoke where lasting freedoms be;
Which breaks the clouds and opens forth the light,
  That doth both shine and give us sight to see.
O take fast hold; let that light be thy guide
  In this small course which birth draws out to death,
And think how evil becometh him to slide,
  Who seeketh heaven, and comes of heavenly breath.
    Then farewell, world; thy uttermost I see;
    Eternal Love, maintain thy life in me.

Sir Philip Sidney

44

Look, Delia, how w' esteem the half-blown rose,
  The image of thy blush, and summer's honour,
Whilst yet her tender bud doth undisclose
  That full of beauty Time bestows upon her.
No sooner spreads her glory in the air
  But straight her wide-blown pomp comes to decline;
She then is scorn'd that late adorn'd the fair:
  So fade the roses of those cheeks of thine.
No April can revive thy withered flowers,
  Whose springing grace adorns thy glory now;
Swift, speedy Time, feather'd with flying hours,
  Dissolves the beauty of the fairest brow.
    Then do not thou such treasure waste in vain,
    But love now, whilst thou mayst be lov'd again.

Samuel Daniel

45

But love whilst that thou mayst be lov'd again,
  Now whilst thy May hath fill'd thy lap with flowers,
Now whilst thy beauty bears without a stain;
  Now use the summer smiles ere winter lours.
And whilst thou spread'st unto the rising sun
  The fairest flower that ever saw the light,
Now joy thy time before thy sweet be done:
  And, Delia, think thy morning must have night,
And that thy brightness sets at length to west,
  When thou wilt close up that which now thou show'st;
And think the same becomes thy fading best,
  Which then shall most enveil and shadow most.
    Men do not weigh the stalk for what it was,
    When once they find her flower, her glory, pass.

Samuel Daniel

46

When men shall find thy flower, thy glory, pass,
  And thou with careful brow sitting alone
Received hast this message from thy glass,
  That tells the truth and says that all is gone,
Fresh shalt thou see in me the wounds thou madest,
  Though spent thy flame, in me the heat remaining;
I that have lov'd thee thus before thou fadest,
  My faith shall wax, when thou art in thy waning.
The world shall find this miracle in me,
  That fire can burn when all the matter's spent;
Then what my faith hath been thyself shalt see,
  And that thou wast unkind thou mayst repent.
    Thou mayst repent that thou hast scorn'd my tears,
    When winter snows upon thy sable hairs.

Samuel Daniel

47

When winter snows upon thy sable hairs,
  And frost of age hath nipp'd thy beauties near;
When dark shall seem thy day that never clears,
  And all lies wither'd that was held so dear;
Then take this picture which I here present thee,
  Limned with a pencil not all unworthy;
Here see the gifts that God and Nature lent thee;
  Here read thyself, and what I suffer'd for thee.
This may remain thy lasting monument,
  Which happily posterity may cherish;
These colours with thy fading are not spent;
  These may remain when thou and I shall perish.
    If they remain, then thou shalt live thereby;
    They will remain, and so thou canst not die.

Samuel Daniel

48

Care-charmer Sleep, son of the sable Night,
  Brother to Death, in silent darkness born,
Relieve my languish, and restore the light,
  With dark forgetting of my care's return.
And let the day be time enough to mourn
  The shipwreck of my ill-adventured youth;
Let waking eyes suffice to wail their scorn,
  Without the torment of the night's untruth.
Cease, dreams, the images of day-desires,
  To model forth the passions of the morrow;
Never let rising sun approve you liars,
  To add more grief to aggravate my sorrow.
    Still let me sleep, embracing clouds in vain;
    And never wake to feel the day's disdain.

Samuel Daniel

49

Fair sun, if you would have me praise your light,
When night approacheth, wherefore do you flee?
Time is so short, beauties so many be,
As I have need to see them day and night,
That by continual view my verses might
Tell all the beams of your divinity;
Which praise to you and joy should be to me,
You living by my verse, I by your sight.
I by your sight, and not you by my verse;
Need mortal skill immortal praise rehearse?
No, no, though eyes were blind, and verse were dumb
Your beauty should be seen and your fame known;
For by the wind which from my sighs doth come,
Your praises round about the world are blown.

Henry Constable

50

Miracle of the world! I never will deny
That former poets praise the beauty of their days;
But all those beauties were but figures of thy praise,
And all those poets did of thee but prophesy.
Thy coming to the world hath taught us to descry
What Petrarch's Laura meant, for truth the lips bewrays
Lo! why th'Italians, yet which never saw thy rays,
To find out Petrarch's sense such forged glosses try.
The beauties, which he in a veil enclos'd beheld,
But revelations were within his secret heart,
By which in parables thy coming he foretold;
His songs were hymns of thee, which only now befo
Thy image should be sung; for thou that goddess art,
Which only we without idolatry adore.

Henry Constable

51

In that, O Queen of queens, thy birth was free
From guilt, which others doth of grace bereave,
When in their mother's womb they life receive,
God as his sole-born daughter loved thee.
To match thee like thy birth's nobility,
He thee his Spirit for thy spouse did leave,
Of whom thou didst his only Son conceive,
And so wast link'd to all the Trinity.
Cease then, O queens, who earthly crowns do wear,
To glory in the pomp of worldly things!
If men such high respect unto you bear,
Which daughters wives and mothers are of kings,
What honour should unto that Queen be done,
Who had your God for father, spouse and son?

Henry Constable

52

To Saint Mary Magdalen

Blessed offender, who thyself hast tried
How far a sinner differs from a saint,
Join thy wet eyes with tears of my complaint,
While I sigh for that grave for which thou cried.
No longer let my sinful soul abide
In fever of thy first desires faint;
But let that love, which last thy heart did taint
With pangs of thy repentance, pierce my side.
So shall my soul no foolish virgin be
With empty lamp; but like a Magdalen bear
For ointment box a breast with oil of grace:
And so the zeale, which then shall burn in me,
May make my heart like to a lamp appear,
And in my spouse's palace give me place.

Henry Constable

53

Behold, dear mistress, how each pleasant green
Will now renew his summer's livery:
The fragrant flowers which have not long been seen
Will flourish now ere long in bravery.
But I, alas, within whose mourning mind
The grafts of grief are only given to grow,
Cannot enjoy the spring which others find,
But still my will must wither all in woe.
The lusty Ver that whilom might exchange
My grief to joy, and my delight increase,
Springs now elsewhere and shows to me but strange;
My winter's woe, therefore, can never cease.
In other coasts his sun doth clearly shine,
And comfort lend to every mould but mine.

Thomas Watson

54

Like to a hermit poor in place obscure
I mean to spend my days of endless doubt,
To wail such woes as time cannot recure,
Where none but death shall ever find me out.

My food shall be of care and sorrow made,
My drink nought else but tears fall'n from mine eyes;
And for my light in such obscured shade
The flames shall serve that from my heart arise.

A gown of grey my body shall attire,
My staff of broken hope whereon I'll stay;
Of late repentance link'd with long desire
The couch is fram'd whereon my limbs I'll lay;

And at my gate despair shall linger still
To let in death when love and fortune will.

Sir Walter Ralegh (?)

55

Like truthless dreams, so are my joys expired,
And past return are all my dandled days;
My love misled, and fancy quite retired,
Of all which past, the sorrow only stays.

My lost delights, now clean from sight of land,
Have left me all alone in unknown ways;
My mind to woe, my life in fortune's hand,
Of all which past, the sorrow only stays.

As in a country strange without companion,
I only wail the wrong of death's delays,
Whose sweet spring spent, whose summer well nigh done,
Of all which past, the sorrow only stays;

Whom care forewarns, ere age and winter cold,
To haste me hence, to find my fortune's fold.

Sir Walter Ralegh

56

Ah, sweet Content! where is thy mild abode?
Is it with shepherds and light-hearted swains,
Which sing upon the downs, and pipe abroad,
Tending their flocks and cattle on the plains?
Ah, sweet Content! where dost thou safely rest?
In heaven with angels which the praises sing
Of him that made, and rules at his behest,
The minds and hearts of every living thing?
Ah, sweet Content! where doth thine harbour hold?
Is it in churches, with religious men,
Which please the gods with prayers manifold,
And in their studies meditate it then?
Whether thou dost in heaven or earth appear,
Be where thou wilt, thou wilt not harbour here.

Barnabe Barnes

57

A blast of wind, a momentary breath,
  A wat'ry bubble symboliz'd with air,
  A sun-blown rose, but for a season fair,
A ghostly glance, a skeleton of death,
A morning dew pearling the grass beneath,
  Whose moisture sun's appearance doth impair,
  A lightning glimpse, a muse of thought and care,
A planet's shot, a shade which followeth;
A voice which vanisheth so soon as heard,
  The thriftless heir of time, a rolling wave,
A show no more in action than regard,
  A mass of dust, world's momentary slave,
    Is man in state of our old Adam made,
    Soon born to die, soon flourishing to fade.

Barnabe Barnes

58

Like Memnon's rock, touch'd with the rising sun,
Which yields a sound and echoes forth a voice;
But, when it's drown'd in western seas, is done,
And drowsy-like leaves off to make a noise:
So I, my Love, enlight'ned with your shine,
A poet's skill within my soul I shroud,
Not rude like that which finer wits decline,
But such as Muses to the best allow'd:
But when your figure and your shape is gone,
I speechless am, like as I was before;
Or if I write, my verse is fill'd with moan,
And blurr'd with tears, by falling in such store:
  Then muse not, Licia, if my Muse be slack,
  For when I wrote I did thy beauty lack.

Giles Fletcher

59

Not causeless were you christen'd, gentle flowers,
The one of faith, the other fancy's pride,
For she who guides both faith and fancy's power
In your fair colours wraps her ivory side.
As one of you hath whiteness without stain,
So spotless is my love and never tainted;
And as the other shadoweth faith again,
Such is my lass, with no fond change acquainted:
And as nor tyrant sun nor winter weather
May ever change sweet Amaranthus' hue,
So she though love and fortune join together
Will never leave to be both fair and true.
 And should I leave thee then, thou pretty elf?
 Nay, first let Damon quite forget himself.

Thomas Lodge

60

Muses that sing Love's sensual empery,
 And lovers kindling your enraged fires
At Cupid's bonfires burning in the eye,
 Blown with the empty breath of vain desires;
You that prefer the painted cabinet
 Before the wealthy jewels it doth store ye,
That all your joys in dying figures set,
 And stain the living substance of your glory:
Abjure those joys, abhor their memory,
 And let my love the honoured subject be
 Of love, and honour's complete history;
Your eyes were never yet let in to see
 The majesty and riches of the mind,
 But dwell in darkness; for your God is blind.

George Chapman

61

The merry cuckoo, messenger of Spring,
  His trumpet shrill hath thrice already sounded;
That warns all lovers wait upon their king,
  Who now is coming forth with garland crowned:
  With noise whereof the quire of birds resounded
Their anthems sweet devised of love's praise,
  That all the woods their echoes back rebounded,
As if they knew the meaning of their lays.
But 'mongst them all, which did love's honour raise,
  No word was heard of her that most it ought,
But she his precept proudly disobeys,
  And doth his idle message set at nought.
    Therefore, O love, unless she turn to thee
    Ere cuckoo end, let her a rebel be.

Edmund Spenser

62

After long storms and tempests' sad assay,
  Which hardly I endured heretofore,
In dread of death and dangerous dismay,
  With which my silly bark was tossed sore,
  I do at length descry the happy shore,
In which I hope ere long for to arrive;
  Fair soil it seems from far and fraught with store
Of all that dear and dainty is alive.
Most happy he that can at last achieve
  The joyous safety of so sweet a rest;
Whose least delight sufficeth to deprive
  Remembrance of all pains which him oppress'd.
    All pains are nothing in respect of this,
    All sorrows short that gain eternal bliss.

Edmund Spenser

63

Most glorious Lord of life, that on this day
  Didst make thy triumph over death and sin;
And, having harrow'd hell, didst bring away
  Captivity thence captive, us to win:
  This joyous day, dear Lord, with joy begin;
And grant that we, for whom thou didest die,
  Being with thy dear blood clean wash'd from sin,
May live for ever in felicity.
And that thy love we weighing worthily,
  May likewise love thee for the same again;
And for thy sake, that all like dear didst buy,
  With love may one another entertain.
    So let us love, dear Love, like as we ought;
    Love is the lesson which the Lord us taught.

Edmund Spenser

64

Fresh Spring, the herald of love's mighty king,
  In whose coat armour richly are displayed
All sorts of flowers the which on earth do spring
  In goodly colours gloriously arrayed;
  Go to my love, where she is careless laid,
Yet in her winter's bower not well awake;
  Tell her the joyous time will not be stayed
Unless she do him by the forelock take.
Bid her therefore herself soon ready make,
  To wait on Love amongst his lovely crew;
Where every one that misseth then her make
  Shall be by him amerc'd with penance due.
    Make haste therefore, sweet love, whilst it is prime,
    For none can call again the passed time.

Edmund Spencer

65

One day I wrote her name upon the strand,
  But came the waves and washed it away:
Again I wrote it with a second hand,
  But came the tide and made my pains his prey.
  'Vain man,' said she, 'that dost in vain essay
A mortal thing so to immortalize;
  For I myself shall like to this decay,
And eke my name be wiped out likewise.'
'Not so,' quod I, 'let baser things devise
  To die in dust, but you shall live by fame;
My verse your virtues rare shall eternize,
  And in the heavens write your glorious name:
    Where, whenas Death shall all the world subdue
    Our love shall live, and later life renew.'

Edmund Spenser

66

An evil spirit, your beauty, haunts me still,
  Wherewith, alas, I have been long possessed,
Which ceaseth not to tempt me to each ill,
  Nor gives me once but one poor minute's rest;
In me it speaks, whether I sleep or wake,
  And when by means to drive it out I try,
With greater torments then it me doth take,
  And tortures me in most extremity;
Before my face it lays down my despairs,
  And hastes me on unto a sudden death,
Now tempting me to drown myself in tears,
  And then in sighing to give up my breath.
    Thus am I still provok'd to every evil
    By this good wicked spirit, sweet angel devil.

Michael Drayton

67

Why should your fair eyes with such sovereign grace
  Disperse their rays on every vulgar spirit,
Whilst I in darkness in the self-same place
  Get not one glance to recompense my merit?
So doth the ploughman gaze the wandering star,
  And only rest contented with the light,
That never learn'd what constellations are,
  Beyond the bent of his unknowing sight.
O! why should beauty, custom to obey,
  To their gross sense apply herself so ill?
Would God I were as ignorant as they,
  When I am made unhappy by my skill;
    Only compell'd on this poor good to boast,
    Heavens are not kind to them that know them most.

Michael Drayton

68

How many paltry, foolish, painted things,
  That now in coaches trouble every street,
Shall be forgotten, whom no poet sings,
  Ere they be well wrapp'd in their winding-sheet?
Where I to thee eternity shall give,
  When nothing else remaineth of these days,
And queens hereafter shall be glad to live
  Upon the alms of thy superfluous praise.
Virgins and matrons reading these my rhymes,
  Shall be so much delighted with thy story,
That they shall grieve they liv'd not in these times,
  To have seen thee, their sex's only glory.
    So shalt thou fly above the vulgar throng,
    Still to survive in my immortal song.

Michael Drayton

69

Since there's no help, come let us kiss and part.
  Nay, I have done; you get no more of me,
And I am glad, yea, glad with all my heart,
  That thus so cleanly I myself can free;
Shake hands for ever, cancel all our vows,
  And when we meet at any time again,
Be it not seen in either of our brows
  That we one jot of former love retain.
Now at the last gasp of Love's latest breath,
  When, his pulse failing, Passion speechless lies,
When Faith is kneeling by his bed of death,
  And Innocence is closing up his eyes,
    Now if thou wouldst, when all have given him over,
    From death to life thou might'st him yet recover.

Michael Drayton

70

Let others of the world's decaying tell:
  I envy not those of the golden age
  That did their careless thoughts for nought engage
But, cloy'd with all delights, liv'd long and well.
And, as for me, I mind t'applaud my fate:
  Though I was long in coming to the light,
  Yet may I mount to fortune's highest height;
So great a good could never come too late.
  I'm glad that it was not my chance to live
Till as that heavenly creature first was born,
Who as an angel doth the earth adorn,
  And buried virtue in the tomb revive:
    For vice o'erflows the world with such a flood,
    That in it all, save she, there is no good.

William Alexander, Earl of Stirling

71

Shall I compare thee to a summer's day?
Thou art more lovely and more temperate:
Rough winds do shake the darling buds of May,
And summer's lease hath all too short a date:
Sometime too hot the eye of heaven shines,
And often is his gold complexion dimm'd;
And every fair from fair sometime declines,
By chance, or nature's changing course untrimm'd;
But thy eternal summer shall not fade,
Nor lose possession of that fair thou ow'st,
Nor shall death brag thou wander'st in his shade,
When in eternal lines to time thou grow'st;
So long as men can breathe, or eyes can see,
So long lives this, and this gives life to thee.

William Shakespeare

72

When in disgrace with fortune and men's eyes
I all alone beweep my outcast state,
And trouble deaf heaven with my bootless cries,
And look upon myself, and curse my fate,
Wishing me like to one more rich in hope,
Featur'd like him, like him with friends possess'd,
Desiring this man's art, and that man's scope,
With what I most enjoy contented least;
Yet in these thoughts myself almost despising,
Haply I think on thee, and then my state,
Like to the lark at break of day arising
From sullen earth, sings hymns at heaven's gate;
For thy sweet love rememb'red such wealth brings
That then I scorn to change my state with kings.

William Shakespeare

73

When to the sessions of sweet silent thought
I summon up remembrance of things past,
I sigh the lack of many a thing I sought,
And with old woes new wail my dear time's waste:
Then can I drown an eye, unus'd to flow,
For precious friends hid in death's dateless night,
And weep afresh love's long-since-cancell'd woe,
And moan the expense of many a vanish'd sight:
Then can I grieve at grievances foregone,
And heavily from woe to woe tell o'er
The sad account of fore-bemoaned moan,
Which I new pay as if not paid before.
But if the while I think on thee, dear friend,
All losses are restor'd and sorrows end.

William Shakespeare

74

Not marble, nor the gilded monuments
Of princes, shall outlive this powerful rhyme;
But you shall shine more bright in these contents
Than unswept stone, besmear'd with sluttish time.
When wasteful war shall statues overturn,
And broils root out the work of masonry,
Nor Mars his sword nor war's quick fire shall burn
The living record of your memory.
'Gainst death and all oblivious enmity
Shall you pace forth; your praise shall still find room
Even in the eyes of all posterity
That wear this world out to the ending doom.
So, till the judgement that yourself arise,
You live in this, and dwell in lovers' eyes.

William Shakespeare

75

Since brass, nor stone, nor earth, nor boundless sea,
But sad mortality o'er-sways their power,
How with this rage shall beauty hold a plea
Whose action is no stronger than a flower?
Oh! how shall summer's honey breath hold out
Against the wrackful siege of battering days,
When rocks impregnable are not so stout,
Nor gates of steel so strong, but Time decays?
O fearful meditation! where, alack,
Shall Time's best jewel from Time's chest lie hid?
Or what strong hand can hold his swift foot back?
Or who his spoil of beauty can forbid?
Oh, none, unless this miracle have might,
That in black ink my love may still shine bright.

William Shakespeare

76

Tir'd with all these, for restful death I cry;
As to behold desert a beggar born,
And needy nothing trimm'd in jollity,
And purest faith unhappily forsworn,
And gilded honour shamefully misplaced,
And maiden virtue rudely strumpeted,
And right perfection wrongfully disgraced,
And strength by limping sway disabled,
And art made tongue-tied by authority,
And folly, doctor-like, controlling skill,
And simple truth miscall'd simplicity,
And captive good attending captain ill.
  Tir'd with all these, from these would I be gone,
  Save that, to die, I leave my Love alone.

William Shakespeare

77

No longer mourn for me when I am dead,
Than you shall hear the surly sullen bell
Give warning to the world that I am fled
From this vile world, with vilest worms to dwell:
Nay, if you read this line, remember not
The hand that writ it; for I love you so,
That I in your sweet thoughts would be forgot,
If thinking on me then should make you woe.
O! if, I say, you look upon this verse,
When I perhaps compounded am with clay,
Do not so much as my poor name rehearse,
But let your love even with my life decay;
 Lest the wise world should look into your moan,
 And mock you with me after I am gone.

William Shakespeare

78

That time of year thou mayst in me behold
When yellow leaves, or none, or few, do hang
Upon those boughs which shake against the cold,
Bare ruin'd choirs, where late the sweet birds sang.
In me thou see'st the twilight of such day
As after sunset fadeth in the west;
Which by and by black night doth take away,
Death's second self, that seals up all in rest.
In me thou see'st the glowing of such fire,
That on the ashes of his youth doth lie,
As the death-bed whereon it must expire,
Consum'd with that which it was nourish'd by.
 This thou perceiv'st, which makes thy love more strong
 To love that well which thou must leave ere long.

William Shakespeare

79

They that have power to hurt and will do none,
That do not do the thing they most do show,
Who, moving others, are themselves as stone,
Unmoved, cold, and to temptation slow;
They rightly do inherit heaven's graces,
And husband nature's riches from expense;
They are the lords and owners of their faces,
Others but stewards of their excellence.
The summer's flower is to the summer sweet,
Though to itself it only live and die,
But if that flower with base infection meet,
The basest weed outbraves his dignity:
For sweetest things turn sourest by their deeds;
Lilies that fester smell far worse than weeds.

William Shakespeare

80

To me, fair friend, you never can be old,
For as you were when first your eye I eyed,
Such seems your beauty still. Three winters cold
Have from the forests shook three summers' pride;
Three beauteous springs to yellow autumn turned
In process of the seasons have I seen,
Three April perfumes in three hot Junes burned,
Since first I saw you fresh, which yet are green.
Ah! yet doth beauty, like a dial-hand,
Steal from his figure, and no pace perceived;
So your sweet hue, which methinks still doth stand,
Hath motion, and mine eye may be deceived.
For fear of which, hear this, thou age unbred;
Ere you were born was beauty's summer dead.

William Shakespeare

81

Let me not to the marriage of true minds
Admit impediments. Love is not love
Which alters when it alteration finds,
Or bends with the remover to remove.
O, no! it is an ever-fixed mark,
That looks on tempests and is never shaken;
It is the star to every wandering bark,
Whose worth's unknown, although his height be taken
Love's not Time's fool, though rosy lips and cheeks
Within his bending sickle's compass come;
Love alters not with his brief hours and weeks,
But bears it out even to the edge of doom.
If this be error, and upon me proved,
I never writ, nor no man ever loved.

William Shakespeare

82

Th'expense of spirit in a waste of shame
Is lust in action; and till action, lust
Is perjur'd, murd'rous, bloody, full of blame,
Savage, extreme, rude, cruel, not to trust;
Enjoy'd no sooner but despised straight;
Past reason hunted, and, no sooner had,
Past reason hated, as a swallowed bait,
On purpose laid to make the taker mad;
Made in pursuit and in possession so;
Had, having, and in quest to have, extreme;
A bliss in proof, and prov'd a very woe;
Before a joy propos'd, behind a dream;
All this the world well knows yet none knows well:
To shun the heaven that leads men to this hell.

William Shakespeare

83

My mistress' eyes are nothing like the sun;
Coral is far more red than her lips' red;
If snow be white, why then her breasts are dun;
If hairs be wires, black wires grow on her head.
I have seen roses damaskt, red and white,
But no such roses see I in her cheeks;
And in some perfume is there more delight
Than in the breath that from my mistress reeks.
I love to hear her speak, yet well I know
That music hath a far more pleasing sound;
I grant I never saw a goddess go;
My mistress when she walks treads on the ground:
  And yet by heaven I think my love as rare
  As any she belied with false compare.

William Shakespeare

84

Poor soul, the centre of my sinful earth,
Feeding these rebel powers that thee array,
Why dost thou pine within and suffer dearth,
Painting thy outward walls so costly gay?
Why so large cost, having so short a lease,
Dost thou upon thy fading mansion spend?
Shall worms, inheritors of this excess,
Eat up thy charge? Is this thy body's end?
Then, soul, live thou upon thy servant's loss,
And let that pine to aggravate thy store;
Buy terms divine, in selling hours of dross;
Within be fed, without be rich no more;
  So shalt thou feed on Death, that feeds on men,
  And Death once dead, there's no more dying then.

William Shakespeare

85

Sleep, Silence' child, sweet father of soft Rest,
  Prince whose approach peace to all mortals brings,
  Indifferent host to shepherds and to kings,
Sole comforter of minds with grief oppress'd.
  Lo! by thy charming rod all breathing things
Lie slumb'ring, with forgetfulness possess'd;
  And yet o'er me to spread thy drowsy wings
Thou spares, alas, who cannot be thy guest.
Since I am thine, O come, but with that face
  To inward light which thou art wont to show,
  With feigned solace ease a true-felt woe,
Or if, deaf god, thou do deny that grace,
  Come as thou wilt, and what thou wilt bequeath:
  I long to kiss the image of my death.

William Drummond

86

The last and greatest herald of heaven's King,
  Girt with rough skins, hies to the deserts wild,
Among that savage brood the woods forth bring,
  Which he than man more harmless found and mild.
His food was blossoms, and what young doth spring,
  With honey that from virgin hives distill'd;
Parch'd body, hollow eyes, some uncouth thing
  Made him appear, long since from earth exil'd.
There burst he forth: "All ye, whose hopes rely
  On God, with mee amidst these deserts mourn;
  Repent, repent, and from old errors turn."
Who listen'd to his voice, obey'd his cry?
  Only the echoes which he made relent
  Rung from their marble caves, *repent, repent.*

William Drummond

87

At the round earth's imagin'd corners, blow
Your trumpets, Angels, and arise, arise
From death, you numberless infinities
Of souls, and to your scatter'd bodies go:
All whom the flood did, and fire shall o'erthrow,
All whom war, dearth, age, agues, tyrannies,
Despair, law, chance, hath slain, and you whose eyes
Shall behold God, and never taste death's woe.
But let them sleep, Lord, and me mourn a space,
For if above all these my sins abound,
'Tis late to ask abundance of thy grace
When we are there: here on this lowly ground
Teach me how to repent, for that's as good
As if thou'dst seal'd my pardon with thy blood.

John Donne

88

Death, be not proud, though some have called thee
Mighty and dreadful, for thou art not so;
For those whom thou think'st thou dost overthrow
Die not, poor Death, nor yet canst thou kill me.
From rest and sleep, which but thy pictures be,
Much pleasure, then from thee much more must flow,
And soonest our best men with thee do go,
Rest of their bones, and soul's delivery.
Thou art slave to Fate, Chance, kings, and desperate men,
And dost with poison, war, and sickness dwell;
And poppy or charms can make us sleep as well,
And better than thy stroke: why swell'st thou then?
One short sleep past, we wake eternally,
And death shall be no more: Death, thou shalt die.

John Donne

89

Batter my heart, three-person'd God; for you
As yet but knock, breathe, shine, and seek to mend;
That I may rise and stand, o'erthrow me, and bend
Your force to break, blow, burn, and make me new.
I, like an usurp'd town, to another due,
Labour t'admit you, but Oh, to no end:
Reason, your viceroy in me, me should defend,
But is captiv'd, and proves weak or untrue.
Yet dearly I love you, and would be loved fain,
But am betroth'd unto your enemy:
Divorce me, untie, or break that knot again;
Take me to you, imprison me, for I,
Except you enthrall me, never shall be free,
Nor ever chaste, except you ravish me.

John Donne

90

Oh, to vex me, contraries meet in one!
Inconstancy unnaturally hath begot
A constant habit; that when I would not
I change in vows and in devotion.
As humorous is my contrition
As my profane love, and as soon forgot;
As riddlingly distemper'd, cold and hot,
As praying, as mute, as infinite, as none.
I durst not view heaven yesterday; and to-day
In prayers and flattering speeches I court God;
To-morrow I quake with true fear of his rod.
So my devout fits come and go away
Like a fantastic ague; save that here
Those are my best days when I shake with fear.

John Donne

91

Love is the peace whereto all thoughts do strive,
Done and begun with all our powers in one;
The first and last in us that is alive,
End of the good, and therewith pleas'd alone;
Perfection's spirit, Goddess of the mind,
Passed through hope, desire, grief and fear;
A simple goodness in the flesh refin'd,
Which of the joys to come doth witness bear;
Constant, because it sees no cause to vary,
A quintessence of passions overthrown.
Rais'd above all that change of objects carry,
A nature by no other nature known:
  For Glory's of eternity a frame,
  That by all bodies else obscures her name.

Fulke Greville, Lord Brooke

92

The earth with thunder torn, with fire blasted,
With waters drowned, with windy palsy shaken,
Cannot for this with heaven be distasted,
Since thunder, rain and winds from earth are taken.
Man torn with love, with inward furies blasted,
Drown'd with despair, with fleshly lustings shaken,
Cannot for this with heaven be distasted:
Love, fury, lustings out of man are taken.
Then Man, endure thy self, those clouds will vanish;
Life is a top which whipping sorrow driveth;
Wisdom must bear what our flesh cannot banish;
The humble lead, the stubborn bootless striveth:
  Or Man, forsake thy self, to heaven turn thee;
  Her flames enlighten nature, never burn thee.

Fulke Greville, Lord Brooke

POEMS FROM PROSE WORKS

93

Ah! were she pitiful as she is fair,
  Or but as mild as she is seeming so,
Then were my hopes greater than my despair;
  Then all the world were heaven, nothing woe.
Ah! were her heart relenting as her hand,
  That seems to melt even with the mildest touch,
Then knew I where to seat me in a land
  Under the wide heavens—but yet not such.
So as she shews, she seems the budding rose,
  Yet sweeter far than is an earthly flower;
Sovereign of beauty, like the spray she grows,
  Compass'd she is with thorns and cankered flower;
Yet were she willing to be pluck'd and worn,
She would be gathered, though she grew on thorn.

Ah! when she sings, all music else be still,
  For none must be compared to her note;
Ne'er breath'd such glee from Philomela's bill,
  Nor from the morning singer's swelling throat.
Ah! when she riseth from her blissful bed,
  She comforts all the world, as doth the sun;
And at her sight the night's foul vapour's fled;
  When she is set, the gladsome day is done.
O glorious sun! imagine me the west,
Shine in my arms, and set thou in my breast.

Robert Greene

94

Weep not, my wanton, smile upon my knee;
When thou art old there's grief enough for thee.
Mother's wag, pretty boy,
Father's sorrow, father's joy;
When thy father first did see
Such a boy by him and me,
He was glad, I was woe;
Fortune chang'd made him so,
When he left his pretty boy,
Last his sorrow, first his joy.

Weep not, my wanton, smile upon my knee;
When thou art old there's grief enough for thee.
Streaming tears that never stint,
Like pearl-drops from a flint,
Fell by course from his eyes,
That one another's place supplies;
Thus he griev'd in every part,
Tears of blood fell from his heart,
When he left his pretty boy,
Father's sorrow, father's joy.

Weep not, my wanton, smile upon my knee;
When thou art old there's grief enough for thee.
The wanton smil'd, father wept;
Mother cried, baby leapt;
More he crow'd, more we cried,
Nature could not sorrow hide.
He must go, he must kiss
Child and mother, baby bliss:
For he left his pretty boy,
Father's sorrow, father's joy.
Weep not, my wanton, smile upon my knee;
When thou art old there's grief enough for thee.

Robert Greene

95

My true love hath my heart and I have his,
By just exchange one for another given;
I hold his dear, and mine he cannot miss;
There never was a better bargain driven.
My true love hath my heart and I have his.

His heart in me keeps him and me in one,
My heart in him his thoughts and senses guides;
He loves my heart, for once it was his own;
I cherish his, because in me it bides.
My true love hath my heart and I have his.

Sir Philip Sidney

96

Love in my bosom like a bee
Doth suck his sweet;
Now with his wings he plays with me,
Now with his feet.
Within mine eyes he makes his nest,
His bed amidst my tender breast;
My kisses are his daily feast;
And yet he robs me of my rest.
Ah, wanton, will ye?

And if I sleep, then percheth he
With pretty flight,
And makes his pillow of my knee
The livelong night.
Strike I my lute, he tunes the string;
He music plays if so I sing;
He lends me every lovely thing;
Yet cruel he my heart doth sting.
Whist, wanton, still ye!

Else I with roses every day
  Will whip you hence;
And bind you, when you long to play,
  For your offence.
I'll shut mine eyes to keep you in.
I'll make you fast it for your sin,
I'll count your power not worth a pin.
Alas! what hereby shall I win
  If he gainsay me?

What if I beat the wanton boy
  With many a rod?
He will repay me with annoy,
  Because a god.
Then sit thou safely on my knee,
And let thy bower my bosom be;
Lurk in mine eyes, I like of thee.
O Cupid, so thou pity me,
  Spare not, but play thee.

Thomas Lodge

97

First shall the heavens want starry light,
  The seas be robbed of their waves;
The day want sun, and sun want bright;
  The night want shade, the dead men graves;
    The April, flowers and leaf and tree,
    Before I false my faith to thee.

First shall the tops of highest hills
  By humble plains be overpried;
And poets scorn the Muses' quills,
  And fish forsake the water-glide;
    And Iris lose her coloured weed,
    Before I fail thee at thy need.

First direful hate shall turn to peace,
  And love relent in deep disdain;
And death his fatal stroke shall cease,
  And envy pity every pain;
    And pleasure mourn, and sorrow smile.
    Before I talk of any guile.

First time shall stay his stayless race,
  And winter bless his brows with corn,
And snow bemoisten July's face,
  And winter spring, and summer mourn,
    Before my pen, by help of fame,
    Cease to recite thy sacred name.

Thomas Lodge

98

Ah! what is love? It is a pretty thing,
As sweet unto a shepherd as a king,
    And sweeter too:
For kings have cares that wait upon a crown,
And cares can make the sweetest love to frown.
    Ah then, ah then,
If country loves such sweet desires do gain,
What lady would not love a shepherd swain?

His flocks once folded, he comes home at night,
As merry as a king in his delight,
    And merrier too:
For kings bethink them what the state require,
Where shepherds careless carol by the fire.
    Ah then, ah then,
If country loves such sweet desires do gain,
What lady would not love a shepherd swain?

He kisseth first, then sits as blithe to eat
His cream and curds, as doth the king his meat;
And blither too:
For kings have often fears when they do sup,
Where shepherds dread no poison in their cup.
Ah then, ah then,
If country loves such sweet desires do gain,
What lady would not love a shepherd swain?

To bed he goes, as wanton then I ween,
As is a king in dalliance with a queen;
More wanton too:
For kings have many griefs affects to move,
Where shepheards have no greater grief than love:
Ah then, ah then,
If country loves such sweet desires do gain,
What lady would not love a shepherd swain?

Upon his couch of straw he sleeps as sound
As doth the king upon his beds of down;
More sounder too:
For cares cause kings full oft their sleep to spill,
Where weary shepherds lie and snort their fill.
Ah then, ah then,
If country loves such sweet desires do gain,
What lady would not love a shepherd swain?

Thus with his wife he spends the year as blithe
As doth the king at every tide or sithe;
And blither too:
For kings have wars and broils to take in hand,
Where shepherds laugh, and love upon the land.
Ah then, ah then,
If country loves such sweet desires do gain,
What lady would not love a shepherd swain?

Robert Greene

99

Sweet are the thoughts that savour of content,
The quiet mind is richer than a crown;
Sweet are the nights in careless slumber spent,
The poor estate scorns Fortune's angry frown.
Such sweet content, such minds, such sleep, such bliss,
Beggars enjoy, when princes oft do miss.

The homely house that harbours quiet rest,
The cottage that affords no pride nor care,
The mean that 'grees with country music best,
The sweet consort of mirth and music's fare,
Obscured life sets down a type of bliss;
A mind content both crown and kingdom is.

Robert Greene

100

Pluck the fruit and taste the pleasure,
Youthful lordings, of delight;
Whilst occasion gives you seizure,
Feed your fancies and your sight:
After death, when you are gone,
Joy and pleasure is there none.

Here on earth is nothing stable,
Fortune's changes well are known;
Whilst as youth doth then enable,
Let your seeds of joy be sown:
After death, when you are gone,
Joy and pleasure is there none.

Feast it freely with your lovers,
Blithe and wanton sweets do fade;
Whilst that lovely Cupid hovers
Round about this lovely shade:
Sport it freely, one to one;
After death is pleasure none.

Now the pleasant spring allureth,
And both place and time invites:
Out, alas! what heart endureth
To disclaim his sweet delights?
After death, when we are gone,
Joy and pleasure is there none.

Thomas Lodge

101

Fie, fie on blind fancy!
It hinders youth's joy:
Fair virgins, learn by me
To count Love a toy.

When Love learned first the A B C of delight,
And knew no figures, nor conceited phrase,
He simply gave to due desert her right,
He led not lovers in dark winding ways;
He plainly willed to love, or flatly answered no;
But now who lists to prove, shall find it nothing so.

Fie, fie, then, on fancy!
It hinders youth's joy:
Fair virgins, learn by me
To count Love a toy.

For since he learned to use the poet's pen,
He learned likewise with smoothing words to feign,
Witching chaste ears with trothless tongues of men,
And wronged faith with falsehood and disdain.
He gives a promise now, anon he sweareth no;
Who listeth for to prove, shall find his changings so.

Fie fie, then, on fancy!
It hinders youth's Joy:
Fair virgins, learn by me
To count Love a toy.

Robert Greene

102

When I admire the rose,
That nature makes repose
In you the best of many,
More fair and blest than any,
And see how curious art
Hath decked every part,
I think with doubtful view
Whether you be the rose, or the rose is you.

Thomas Lodge

103

Trust not his wanton tears,
  Lest they beguile ye;
Trust not his childish sigh,
  He breatheth slily.
Trust not his touch,
  His feeling may defile ye;
Trust nothing that he doth,
  The wag is wily.
If you suffer him to prate,
You will rue it over-late;
  Beware of him, for he is witty.
Quickly strive the boy to bind,
Fear him not, for he is blind;
  If he get loose, he shows no pity.

Henry Chettle

104

Beauty sat bathing by a spring
  Where fairest shades did hide her;
The winds blew calm, the birds did sing,
  The cool streams ran beside her.

My wanton thoughts entic'd mine eye
  To see what was forbidden:
But better Memory said, fie!
  So vain Desire was chidden.
    Hey nonny, nonny, &c.

Into a slumber then I fell,
  When fond imagination
Seemed to see, but could not tell
  Her feature or her fashion.
But even as babes in dreams do smile,
  And sometimes fall a-weeping,
So I awak'd, as wise this while
  As when I fell a-sleeping.
    Hey nonny, nonny, &c.

Anthony Munday

105

  Rose-cheek'd Laura, come;
Sing thou smoothly with thy beauty's
Silent music, either other
  Sweetly gracing.

  Lovely forms do flow
From concent divinely framed;
Heaven is music, and thy beauty's
  Birth is heav'nly.

  These dull notes we sing
Discords need for helps to grace them;
Only beauty purely loving
  Knows no discord;

But still moves delight,
Like clear springs renew'd by flowing,
Ever perfect, ever in them–
selves eternal.

Thomas Campion

SONGS FROM PLAYS AND MASQUES

106

Farewell, adieu, that court-like life!
  To war we tend to go:
It is good sport to see the strife
  Of soldiers on a row.
    How merrily they forward march,
      These enemies to slay!
    With hey trim and trixy too
      Their banners they display.

Now shall we have the golden cheats
  When others want the same;
And soldiers have full many feats
  Their enemies to tame.
    With coucking here, and booming there
      They break their foes' array;
    And lusty lads amid the fields
      Their ensigns do display.

The drum and flute play lustily,
  The trumpet blows amain,
And vent'rous knights courageously
  Do march before their train,
    With spears in rest so lively dress'd
      In armour bright and gay,
    With hey trim and trixy too
      Their banners they display.

John Pickering

107

Cupid and my Campaspe played
At cards for kisses, Cupid paid;
He stakes his quiver, bow, and arrows,
His mother's doves, and team of sparrows;
Loses them too; then, down he throws
The coral of his lip, the rose
Growing on's cheek (but none knows how);
With these, the crystal of his brow,
And then the dimple of his chin:
All these did my Campaspe win.
At last, he set her both his eyes;
She won, and Cupid blind did rise.
  O Love! has she done this to thee?
  What shall (alas!) become of me?

John Lyly

108

GRANICHUS O! for a bowl of fat Canary,
Rich Palermo, sparkling Sherry,
Some nectar else, from Juno's dairy;
O! these draughts would make us merry.

PSYLLUS O! for a wench (I deal in faces,
And in other daintier things);
Tickled am I with her embraces,
Fine dancing in such fairy rings.

MANES O! for a plump fat leg of mutton,
Veal, lamb, capon, pig, and coney;
None is happy but a glutton,
None an ass but who wants money.

CHORUS. Wines (indeed) and girls are good,
But brave victuals feast the blood;
For wenches, wine, and lusty cheer,
Jove would leap down to surfeit here.

John Lyly

109

OENONE Fair and fair, and twice so fair,
As fair as any may be;
The fairest shepherd on our green,
A Love for any lady.

PARIS Fair and fair, and twice so fair,
As fair as any may be;
Thy Love is fair for thee alone,
And for no other lady.

OENONE My Love is fair, my Love is gay,
As fresh as bin the flowers in May;
And of my Love my roundelay,
My merry, merry, merry roundelay,
Concludes with Cupid's curse:
They that do change old love for new,
Pray gods they change for worse.

TOGETHER They that do change old love for new,
Pray gods they change for worse.

OENONE Fair and fair, and twice so fair,
As fair as any may be;
The fairest shepherd on our green,
A Love for any lady.

PARIS Fair and fair, and twice so fair,
As fair as any may be;
Thy Love is fair for thee alone,
And for no other lady.

OENONE My Love can pipe, my Love can sing,
My Love can many a pretty thing,

And of his lovely praises ring
My merry, merry, merry roundelays.
  Amen to Cupid's curse:
They that do change old love for new,
  Pray gods they change for worse.
TOGETHER They that do change old love for new,
  Pray gods they change for worse.

George Peele

110

My shag-hair Cyclops, come, let's ply
Our Lemnian hammers lustily;
    By my wife's sparrows,
    I swear these arrows
    Shall singing fly
  Through many a wanton's eye.
These headed are with golden blisses,
These silver ones feather'd with kisses,
    But this of lead
    Strikes a clown dead,
    When in a dance
    He falls in a trance,
To see his black-brow lass not buss him,
And then whines out for death t'untruss him.
So, so, our work being done, let's play,
Holiday (boys), cry Holiday!

John Lyly

111

I serve a mistress whiter than the snow,
  Straighter than cedar, brighter than the glass,
Finer in trip and swifter than the roe,
  More pleasant than the field of flowering grass;
More gladsome to my withering joys that fade,
Than winter's sun or summer's cooling shade

Sweeter than swelling grape of ripest wine,
  Softer than feathers of the fairest swan,
Smoother than jet, more stately than the pine,
  Fresher than poplar, smaller than my span,
Clearer than beauty's fiery pointed beam,
Or icy crust of crystal's frozen stream.

Yet is she curster than the bear by kind,
  And harder-hearted than the aged oak,
More glib than oil, more fickle than the wind,
  Stiffer than steel, no sooner bent but broke.
Lo! thus my service is a lasting sore;
Yet will I serve, although I die therefore.

Anthony Munday

112

TELUSA O yes, O yes, if any maid,
Whom leering Cupid has betrayed
To frowns of spite, to eyes of scorn,
And would in madness now see torn
The boy in pieces,
ALL 3 Let her come
Hither, and lay on him her doom.
EUROTA O yes, O yes, has any lost
A heart, which many a sigh hath cost;
Is any cozen'd of a tear,
Which (as a pearl) disdain does wear?
ALL 3 Here stands the thief, let her but come
Hither, and lay on him her doom.

LARISSA Is any one undone by fire,
And turn'd to ashes through desire?
Did ever any lady weep,
Being cheated of her golden sleep,
Stol'n by sick thoughts?

ALL 3 The Pirate's found,
And in her tears he shall be drowned.
Read his indictment, let him hear
What he's to trust to: Boy, give ear!

John Lyly

113

Hot sun, cool fire, temper'd with sweet air,
Black shade, fair nurse, shadow my white hair;
Shine, sun; burn, fire; breathe, air, and ease me;
Black shade, fair nurse, shroud me and please me:
Shadow, my sweet nurse, keep me from burning,
Make not my glad cause cause of mourning.
Let not my beauty's fire
Inflame unstaid desire,
Nor pierce any bright eye
That wandereth lightly.

George Peele

114

Pan's Syrinx was a girl indeed,
Though now she's turn'd into a reed;
From that dear reed Pan's pipe does come,
A pipe that strikes Apollo dumb;
Nor flute, nor lute, nor gittern can
So chant it, as the pipe of Pan;
Cross-garter'd swains, and dairy girls,
With faces smug, and round as pearls,
When Pan's shrill pipe begins to play,
With dancing wear out night and day;
The bagpipe's drone his hum lays by,
When Pan sounds up his minstrelsy;
His minstrelsy! O base! This quill,
Which at my mouth with wind I fill,
Puts me in mind, though her I miss,
That still my Syrinx' lips I kiss.

John Lyly

115

Gently dip, but not too deep,
For fear you make the golden beard to weep.
Fair maiden, white and red,
Comb me smooth, and stroke my head;
And thou shalt have some cockle bread.

Gently dip, but not too deep,
For fear thou make the golden beard to weep.
Fair maiden, white and red,
Comb me smooth, and stroke my head;
And every hair a sheave shall be,
And every sheave a golden tree.

George Peele

116

When as the rye reach to the chin.
And chopcherry, chopcherry ripe within
Strawberries swimming in the cream,
And school-boys playing in the stream;
Then O, then O, then O my true love said
Till that time come again,
She could not live a maid.

George Peele

117

What thing is love? for sure love is a thing.
It is a prick, it is a sting,
It is a pretty, pretty thing;
It is a fire, it is a coal,
Whose flame creeps in at every hole;
And as my wit doth best devise,
Love's dwelling is in ladies' eyes,
From whence do glance love's piercing darts,
That make such holes into our hearts;

And all the world herein accord,
Love is a great and mighty lord;
And when he list to mount so high,
With Venus he in heaven doth lie,
And evermore hath been a god,
Since Mars and she play'd even and odd.

George Peele

118

Spring, the sweet spring, is the year's pleasant king;
Then blooms each thing, then maids dance in a ring
Cold doth not sting, the pretty birds do sing;
  Cuckoo, jug-jug, pu-we, to-witta-woo!

The palm and may make country houses gay,
Lambs frisk and play, the shepherds pipe all day,
And we hear aye birds tune this merry lay:
  Cuckoo, jug-jug, pu-we, to-witta-woo!

The fields breathe sweet, the daisies kiss our feet,
Young lovers meet, old wives a-sunning sit;
In every street these tunes our ears do greet:
  Cuckoo, jug-jug, pu-we, to-witta-woo!
    Spring, the sweet spring!

Thomas Nashe

119

Fair summer droops, droop men and beasts therefore;
So fair a summer look for never more,
All good things vanish, less than in a day,
Peace, plenty, pleasure, suddenly decay.
  Go not yet away, bright soul of the sad year;
  The earth is hell when thou leav'st to appear.

What, shall those flowers, that deck'd thy garland erst,
Upon thy grave be wastefully dispersed?
O trees, consume your sap in sorrow's source;
Streams, turn to tears your tributary course.
Go not yet hence, bright soul of the sad year;
The earth is hell when thou leav'st to appear.

Thomas Nashe

120

Autumn hath all the summer's fruitful treasure;
Gone is our sport, fled is poor Croydon's pleasure.
Short days, sharp days, long nights come on apace,
Ah! who shall hide us from the winter's face?
Cold doth increase, the sickness will not cease,
And here we lie, God knows, with little ease.
From winter, plague, and pestilence, good Lord, deliver us!

London doth mourn, Lambeth is quite forlorn.
Trades cry, woe worth that ever they were born.
The want of term is town and city's harm;
Close chambers we do want, to keep us warm.
Long banished must we live from our friends;
This low-built house will bring us to our ends.
From winter, plague, and pestilence, good Lord deliver us!

Thomas Nashe

121

Adieu, farewell earth's bliss,
This world uncertain is;
Fond are life's lustful joys,
Death proves them all but toys,
None from his darts can fly.
I am sick, I must die.
Lord, have mercy on us!

Rich men, trust not in wealth,
Gold cannot buy you health;
Physic himself must fade,
All things to end are made.
The plague full swift goes by.
I am sick, I must die.
  Lord, have mercy on us!

Beauty is but a flower
Which wrinkles will devour;
Brightness falls from the air,
Queens have died young and fair,
Dust hath clos'd Helen's eye.
I am sick, I must die.
  Lord, have mercy on us!

Strength stoops unto the grave,
Worms feed on Hector brave,
Swords may not fight with fate,
Earth still holds ope her gate.
Come! come! the bells do cry.
I am sick, I must die.
  Lord, have mercy on us!

Wit with his wantonness
Tasteth death's bitterness;
Hell's executioner
Hath no ears for to hear
What vain art can reply.
I am sick, I must die.
Lord, have mercy on us!

Haste, therefore, each degree,
To welcome destiny.

Heaven is our heritage,
Earth but a player's stage;
Mount we unto the sky.
I am sick, I must die.
Lord, have mercy on us!

Thomas Nashe

122

SILENA O Cupid! monarch over kings,
Wherefore hast thou feet and wings?
It is to show how swift thou art,
When thou wound'st a tender heart.
Thy wings being clipp'd, and feet held still,
Thy bow so many could not kill.

ACCIUS It is all one in Venus' wanton school,
Who highest sits, the wise man or the fool.
Fools in Love's college
Have far more knowledge,
To read a woman over,
Than a neat prating lover.
Nay, 'tis confessed
That fools please women best.

John Lyly

123

Virtue's branches wither, virtue pines,
O pity, pity, and alack the time!
Vice doth flourish, vice in glory shines,
Her gilded boughs above the cedar climb.

Vice hath golden cheeks, O pity, pity!
She in every land doth monarchize.
Virtue is exiled from every city,
Virtue is a fool, vice only wise.

O pity, pity! virtue weeping dies.
  Vice laughs to see her faint, alack the time!
This sinks; with painted wings the other flies.
  Alack, that best should fall, and bad should climb!

O pity, pity, pity! mourn, not sing!
Vice is a saint, virtue an underling.
Vice doth flourish, vice in glory shines,
Virtue's branches wither, virtue pines.

Thomas Dekker

124

Art thou poor, yet hast thou golden slumbers?
  O sweet content!
Art thou rich, yet is thy mind perplexed?
  O punishment!
Dost thou laugh to see how fools are vexed
To add to golden numbers, golden numbers?
O sweet content! O sweet content!
  Work apace, apace, apace, apace;
  Honest labour bears a lovely face;
Then hey nonny nonny, hey nonny nonny!

Canst drink the waters of the crisped spring?
  O sweet content!
Swim'st thou in wealth, yet sink'st in thine own tears?
  O punishment!
Then he that patiently want's burden bears
No burden bears, but is a king, a king!
O sweet content! O sweet content!
  Work apace, apace, apace, apace;
  Honest labour bears a lovely face;
Then hey nonny nonny, hey nonny nonny!

Thomas Dekker (?)

125

Golden slumbers kiss your eyes,
Smiles awake you when you rise.
Sleep, pretty wantons, do not cry,
And I will sing a lullaby:
Rock them, rock them, lullaby.

Care is heavy, therefore sleep you;
You are care, and care must keep you.
Sleep, pretty wantons, do not cry,
And I will sing a lullaby:
Rock them, rock them, lullaby.

Thomas Dekker (?)

126

O! the month of May, the merry month of May,
  So frolic, so gay, and so green, so green, so green!
O! and then did I unto my true Love say,
  Sweet Peg, thou shalt be my Summer's Queen.

Now the nightingale, the pretty nightingale,
  The sweetest singer in all the forest's choir,
Entreats thee, sweet Peggy, to hear thy true Love's tale:
  Lo! yonder she sitteth, her breast against a briar.

But O! I spy the cuckoo, the cuckoo, the cuckoo;
  See where she sitteth; come away, my joy:
Come away, I prithee, I do not like the cuckoo
  Should sing where my Peggy and I kiss and toy.

O! the month of May, the merry month of May,
  So frolic, so gay, and so green, so green, so green!
And then did I unto my true Love say,
  Sweet Peg, thou shalt be my Summer's Queen.

Thomas Dekker

127

The nut-brown ale, the nut-brown ale,
Puts down all drink when it is stale!
The toast, the nutmeg, and the ginger
Will make a sighing man a singer.
Ale gives a buffet in the head,
  But ginger under-props the brain;
When ale would strike a strong man dead
  Then nutmeg tempers it again.
The nut-brown ale, the nut-brown ale,
Puts down all drink when it is stale!

John Marston

128

By the moon we sport and play,
With the night begins our day;
As we dance the dew doth fall;
Trip it, little urchins all,
Lightly as the little bee,
Two by two, and three by three,
And about go we, and about go we.

Anonymous

129

Slow, slow, fresh fount, keep time with my salt tears;
  Yet slower, yet; oh, faintly, gentle springs:
List to the heavy part the music bears,
  Woe weeps out her division when she sings.
        Droop herbs and flowers;
        Fall grief in showers;
        Our beauties are not ours:
          Oh, I could still
(Like melting snow upon some craggy hill)
        Drop, drop, drop, drop,
Since Nature's pride is now a wither'd daffodil.

Ben Jonson

130

Queen and huntress, chaste and fair,
  Now the sun is laid to sleep,
Seated in thy silver chair,
  State in wonted manner keep;
    Hesperus entreats thy light,
    Goddess excellently bright.

Earth, let not thy envious shade
  Dare itself to interpose;
Cynthia's shining orb was made
  Heaven to clear when day did close:
    Bless us then with wished sight,
    Goddess excellently bright.

Lay thy bow of pearl apart,
  And thy crystal shining quiver;
Give unto the flying hart
  Space to breathe, how short soever:
    Thou that mak'st a day of night,
    Goddess excellently bright.

Ben Jonson

131

Midnight's bell goes ting, ting, ting, ting, ting,
Then dogs do howl, and not a bird does sing
But the nightingale, and she cries twit, twit, twit.
Owls then on every bough do sit,
Ravens croak on chimneys' tops,
The cricket in the chamber hops,
And the cats cry mew, mew, mew.
The nibbling mouse is not asleep,
But he goes peep, peep, peep, peep, peep,
  And the cats cry mew, mew, mew,
  And still the cats cry mew, mew, mew.

Thomas Middleton

132

Come, my Celia, let us prove,
While we may, the sports of love;
Time will not be ours for ever,
He, at length, our good will sever.
Spend not then his gifts in vain:
Suns that set may rise again;
But if once we lose this light,
'Tis with us perpetual night.
Why should we defer our joys?
Fame and rumour are but toys.
Cannot we delude the eyes
Of a few poor household spies?
Or his easier ears beguile,
Thus removed by our wile?
'Tis no sin love's fruits to steal,
But the sweet thefts to reveal;
To be taken, to be seen,
These have crimes accounted been.

Ben Jonson

133

Pack, clouds, away, and welcome day,
 With night we banish sorrow;
Sweet air, blow soft; mount, lark, aloft,
 To give my Love good-morrow!
Wings from the wind, to please her mind,
 Notes from the lark I'll borrow;
Bird, prune thy wing, nightingale, sing,
 To give my Love good-morrow!
 To give my Love good-morrow
 Notes from them all I'll borrow.

Wake from thy nest, robin-redbreast,
  Sing, birds, in every furrow;
And from each bill, let music shrill
  Give my fair Love good-morrow!
Blackbird and thrush in every bush,
  Stare, linnet, and cock-sparrow,
You pretty elves, amongst yourselves
  Sing my fair Love good-morrow!
  To give my Love good-morrow
  Sing, birds, in every furrow!

Thomas Heywood

134

Come, Sleep, and with thy sweet deceiving
  Lock me in delight awhile!
  Let some pleasing dreams beguile
  All my fancies; that from thence
  I may feel an influence,
All my powers of care bereaving.

Though but a shadow, but a sliding,
  Let me know some little joy.
  We that suffer long annoy
  Are contented with a thought
  Through an idle fancy wrought:
Oh! let my joys have some abiding.

Francis Beaumont

135

Call for the robin-redbreast and the wren,
Since o'er shady groves they hover
And with leaves and flowers do cover
The friendless bodies of unburied men.
Call unto his funeral dole
The ant, the field-mouse, and the mole,

To rear him hillocks that shall keep him warm,
And, when gay tombs are robb'd, sustain no harm:
But keep the wolf far thence, that's foe to men.
For with his nails he'll dig them up again.

John Webster

136

Still to be neat, still to be dress'd,
As you were going to a feast;
Still to be powd'red, still perfum'd:
Lady, it is to be presum'd,
Though art's hid causes are not found,
All is not sweet, all is not sound.

Give me a look, give me a face,
That makes simplicity a grace;
Robes loosely flowing, hair as free:
Such sweet neglect more taketh me
Than all th'adulteries of art;
They strike mine eyes, but not my heart.

Ben Jonson

137

'Tis mirth that fills the veins with blood,
More than wine, or sleep, or food;
Let each man keep his heart at ease;
No man dies of that disease.
He that would his body keep
From diseases, must not weep;
But whoever laughs and sings,
Never he his body brings
Into fevers, gouts, or rheums,
Or lingeringly his lungs consumes;

Or meets with achës in the bone,
Or catarrhs, or griping stone:
But contented lives for aye;
The more he laughs, the more he may.

Francis Beaumont

138

Are they shadows that we see?
  And can shadows pleasure give?
Pleasures only shadows be,
  Cast by bodies we conceive,
And are made the things we deem
In those figures which they seem.

But these pleasures vanish fast
  Which by shadows are express'd:
Pleasures are not, if they last;
  In their passing is their best.
Glory is most bright and gay
In a flash, and so away.

Feed apace then, greedy eyes,
  On the wonder you behold.
Take it sudden as it flies,
  Though you take it not to hold:
When your eyes have done their part,
Thought must length it in the heart.

Samuel Daniel

139

Roses, their sharp spines being gone,
Not royal in their smells alone,
  But in their hue;
Maiden pinks, of odour faint,
Daisies smell-less, yet most quaint,
  And sweet thyme true;

Primrose, firstborn child of Ver,
Merry springtime's harbinger,
With her bells dim;
Oxlips in their cradles growing,
Marigolds on death-beds blowing,
Larks'-heels trim:

All dear Nature's children sweet
Lie 'fore bride and bridegroom's feet,
Blessing their sense.
Not an angel of the air,
Bird melodious or bird fair,
Be absent hence.

The crow, the slanderous cuckoo, nor
The boding raven, nor chough hoar,
Nor chattering pie,
May on our bride-house perch or sing,
Or with them any discord bring,
But from it fly.

William Shakespeare (?)

140

Lay a garland on my hearse
Of the dismal yew;
Maidens, willow branches bear;
Say I died true.

My Love was false, but I was firm
From my hour of birth.
Upon my buried body lay
Lightly, gently, earth.

John Fletcher

141

Shine out, fair Sun, with all your heat,
  Show all your thousand-colour'd light!
Black Winter freezes to his seat;
  The grey wolf howls, he does so bite;
Crookt Age on three knees creeps the street;
  The boneless fish close quaking lies
And eats for cold his aching feet;
  The stars in icicles arise:
Shine out, and make this winter night
Our beauty's Spring, our Prince of Light!

George Chapman (?)

142

Tell me, dearest, what is love?
'Tis a lightning from above;
'Tis an arrow, 'tis a fire,
'Tis a boy they call Desire;
    'Tis a grave
    Gapes to have
Those poor fools that long to prove.

Tell me more, are women true?
Yes, some are, and some as you.
Some are willing, some are strange,
Since you men first taught to change;
    And till troth
    Be in both,
All shall love, to love anew.

Tell me more yet, can they grieve?
Yes, and sicken sore, but live,
And be wise, and delay,
When you men are as wise as they.
    Then I see
    Faith will be
Never till they both believe.

John Fletcher

143

The hours of sleepy night decay apace,
And now warm beds are fitter than this place.
All time is long that is unwilling spent,
But hours are minutes when they yield content.
The gather'd flowers we love that breathe sweet scent,
But loathe them, their sweet odour being spent.
It is a life is never ill
To lie and sleep in roses still.

The rarer pleasure is, it is more sweet;
And friends are kindest when they seldom meet.
Who would not hear the nightingale still sing,
Or who grew ever weary of the spring?
The day must have her night, the spring her fall,
All is divided, none is lord of all,
It were a most delightful thing
To live in a perpetual spring.

Thomas Campion (?)

LUTANIST SONGS

144

What pleasure have great princes,
  More dainty to their choice,
Than herdmen wild, who careless
  In quiet life rejoice,
And Fortune's fate not fearing
Sing sweet in summer morning?

Their dealings plain and rightful
  Are void of all deceit;
They never know how spiteful
  It is to kneel and wait
On favourite presumptuous,
Whose pride is vain and sumptuous.

All day their flocks each tendeth;
  At night they take their rest,
More quiet than who sendeth
  His ship into the East,
Where gold and pearl are plenty,
But getting very dainty.

For lawyers and their pleading
  They esteem it not a straw;
They think that honest meaning
  Is of itself a law;
Where conscience judgeth plainly,
They spend no money vainly.

Oh, happy who thus liveth,
  Not caring much for gold,
With clothing which sufficeth
  To keep him from the cold.
Though poor and plain his diet,
Yet merry it is and quiet.

Anonymous

145

Though Amaryllis dance in green
    Like Fairy Queen;
    And sing full clear
Corinna can, with smiling cheer,
Yet since their eyes make heart so sore,
Hey ho! chill love no more.

My sheep are lost for want of food,
    And I so wood
    That all the day
I sit and watch a herd-maid gay,
Who laughs to see me sigh so sore;
Hey ho! chill love no more.

Her loving looks, her beauty bright,
    Is such delight
    That all in vain
I love to like and lose my gain
For her that thanks me not therefore.
Hey ho! chill love no more.

Ah, wanton eyes! my friendly foes
    And cause of woes,
    Your sweet desire
Breeds flames of ice, and freezing fire
Ye scorn to see me weep so sore:
Hey ho! chill love no more.

Love ye who list, I force him not:
Sith God it wot,
The more I wail,
The less my sighs and tears prevail:
What shall I do, but say therefore,
Hey ho! chill love no more.

Anonymous

146

My mind to me a kingdom is,
Such present joys therein I find,
That it excels all other bliss
That world affords or grows by kind.
Though much I want which most would have,
Yet still my mind forbids to crave.

No princely pomp, no wealthy store,
No force to win the victory,
No wily wit to salve a sore,
No shape to feed a loving eye;
To none of these I yield as thrall,
For why my mind doth serve for all.

I see how plenty suffers oft,
And hasty climbers soon do fall;
I see that those which are aloft
Mishap doth threaten most of all;
They get with toil, they keep with fear:
Such cares my mind could never bear.

Content I live, this is my stay,
I seek no more than may suffice;
I press to bear no haughty sway;
Look, what I lack my mind supplies;
Lo! thus I triumph like a king,
Content with that my mind doth bring.

Some have too much, yet still do crave;
  I little have, and seek no more.
They are but poor, though much they have,
  And I am rich with little store.
They poor, I rich; they beg, I give;
They lack, I leave; they pine, I live.

I laugh not at another's loss;
  I grudge not at another's gain;
No worldly waves my mind can toss;
  My state at one doth still remain.
I fear no foe, I fawn no friend;
I loathe not life, nor dread my end.

Some weigh their pleasure by their lust,
  Their wisdom by their rage of will;
Their treasure is their only trust,
  A cloaked craft their store of skill:
But all the pleasure that I find
Is to maintain a quiet mind.

My wealth is health and perfect ease,
  My conscience clear my choice defence;
I neither seek by bribes to please,
  Nor by deceit to breed offence.
Thus do I live; thus will I die;
Would all did so as well as I!

Sir Edward Dyer

147

While that the sun with his beams hot
  Scorched the fruits in vale and mountain,
Philon the shepherd, late forgot,
  Sitting besides a crystal fountain

In shadow of a green oak tree,
Upon his pipe this song played he.
'Adieu love, adieu love, untrue love!
Untrue love, untrue love, adieu love,
Your mind is light, soon lost for new love.

'So long as I was in your sight,
I was as your heart, your soul, your treasure;
But evermore you sobb'd, you sigh'd,
Burning in flames beyond all measure.
Three days endured your love to me,
And it was lost in other three.
Adieu love, adieu love, untrue love!
Untrue love, untrue love, adieu love,
Your mind is light, soon lost for new love.

'Another shepherd you did see,
To whom your heart was soon enchained;
Full soon your love was leapt from me;
Full soon my place he had obtained.
Soon came a third your love to win,
And we were out, and he was in.
Adieu love, adieu love, untrue love!
Untrue love, untrue love, adieu love,
Your mind is light, soon lost for new love.

'Sure you have made me passing glad,
That you your mind so soon removed,
Before that I the leisure had
To choose you for my best beloved;
For all my love was past and done,
Two days before it was begun.
Adieu love, adieu love, untrue love!
Untrue love, untrue love, adieu love,
Your mind is light, soon lost for new love.'

Anonymous

148

Come away, come, sweet Love! The golden morning breaks;
All the earth, all the air, of love and pleasure speaks.
  Teach thine arms then to embrace,
    And sweet rosy lips to kiss,
    And mix our souls in mutual bliss.
  Eyes were made for beauty's grace,
    Viewing, rueing love's long pains,
    Procur'd by beauty's rude disdain.

Come away, come, sweet Love! The golden morning wastes,
While the sun from his sphere his fiery arrows casts,
  Making all the shadows fly,
    Playing, staying, in the grove,
    To entertain the stealth of love.
  Thither, sweet Love, let us hie,
    Flying, dying in desire,
    Wing'd with sweet hopes and heavenly fire.

Come away, come, sweet Love! Do not in vain adorn
Beauty's grace, that should rise like to the naked morn.
  Lilies on the river's side
    And fair Cyprian flowers new-blown
    Desire no beauties but their own,
  Ornament is nurse of pride;
    Pleasure, measure love's delight.
    Haste, then, sweet Love, our wished flight.

Anonymous

149

Dear, if you change, I'll never choose again;
  Sweet, if you shrink, I'll never think of love;
Fair, if you fail, I'll judge all beauty vain;
  Wise, if too weak, mo wits I'll never prove.
Dear, Sweet, Fair, Wise, change, shrink, nor be not weak;
And, on my faith, my faith shall never break.

Earth with her flowers shall sooner heaven adorn;
Heaven her bright stars through earth's dim globe shall move;
Fire heat shall lose, and frosts of flames be born;
Air, made to shine, as black as hell shall prove.
Earth, Heaven, Fire, Air, the world transform'd shall view,
Ere I prove false to faith, or strange to you.

Anonymous

150

Faustina hath the fairer face,
And Phillida the feater grace;
Both have mine eye enriched.
This sings full sweetly with her voice,
Her fingers make as sweet a noise;
Both have mine ear bewitched.
Ay me! sith Fates have so provided,
My heart, alas! must be divided.

Anonymous

151

Take Time while Time doth last,
Mark how Fair fadeth fast,
Beware if Envy reign,
Take heed of proud Disdain.
Hold fast now in thy youth,
Regard thy vowed Truth,
Lest when thou waxeth old,
Friends fail and Love grow cold.

Anonymous

152

Life is a poet's fable,
And all her days are lies
Stolen from Death's reckoning table;
For I die, for I die; as I speak,
Death times the notes that I do break.

Childhood doth die in youth,
  And youth in old age dies.
I thought I liv'd in truth,
But I die, but I die, now I see,
Each age of Death makes one degree.

Farewell the doting score
  Of world's arithmetic.
Life, I'll trust thee no more;
Till I die, till I die, for they sake
I'll go by Death's new almanac.

This instant of my song
  A thousand men lie sick,
A thousand knells are rung;
And I die, and I die as they sing;
They are but dead and I dying.

Death is but Life's decay,
Life time, Time wastes away.
Then reason bids me say
That I die, that I die, though my breath
Prolongs this space of lingering death.

Anonymous

153

She whose matchless beauty staineth
What best judgement fair'st maintaineth,
She, O she, my love disdaineth.

Can a creature so excelling
Harbour scorn in beauty's dwelling,
All kind pity thence expelling?

Pity beauty much commendeth,
And th'embracer oft befriendeth,
When all eye-contentment endeth.

Time proves beauty transitory.
Scorn, the stain of beauty's glory,
In time makes the scorner sorry.

None adores the sun declining,
Love all love falls to resigning,
When the sun of love leaves shining.

So when flower of beauty fails thee,
And age stealing on assails thee,
Then mark what this scorn avails thee.

Then those hearts which now complaining
Feel the wounds of thy disdaining,
Shall contemn thy beauty waning.

Yea, thine own heart, now dear-prized,
Shall, with spite and grief surprised,
Burst to find itself despised.

When like harms have them requited,
Who in others' harms delighted,
Pleasingly the wrong'd are righted.

Such revenge my wrongs attending,
Hope still lives on time depending,
By thy plagues my torments ending.

Anonymous

154

Sweet Philomel, in groves and deserts haunting,
Oft glads my heart and ears with her sweet chanting.
  But then her tunes delight me best,
  When perch'd with prick against her breast,
She sings 'fie, fie,' as if she suffer'd wrong,
Till, seeming pleas'd, 'sweet, sweet' concludes her song.

Sweet Jinny sings and talks and sweetly smileth,
And with her wanton mirth my griefs beguileth.
  But then methinks she pleaseth best
  When, while my hands move love's request,
She cries 'fie, fie,' and, seeming loth, gainsays,
Till, better pleas'd, 'sweet, sweet' content bewrays.

Anonymous

155

Fine knacks for ladies, cheap, choice, brave and new!
  Good pennyworths! but money cannot move.
I keep a fair but for the Fair to view;
  A beggar may be liberal of love.
Though all my wares be trash, the heart is true.

Great gifts are guiles and look for gifts again;
  My trifles come as treasures from my mind.
It is a precious jewel to be plain;
  Sometimes in shell the orient'st pearls we find.
Of others take a sheaf, of me a grain.

Within this pack pins, points, laces, and gloves,
  And divers toys fitting a country fair,
But in my heart, where duty serves and loves,
  Turtles and twins, court's brood, a heavenly pair.
Happy the heart that thinks of no removes!

Anonymous

156

I saw my lady weep,
  And Sorrow proud to be advanced so
In those fair eyes where all perfections keep.
  Her face was full of woe;
But such a woe, believe me, as wins more hearts,
Than Mirth can do with her enticing parts.

Sorrow was there made fair,
  And Passion wise, tears a delightful thing;
Silence beyond all speech a wisdom rare.
  She made her sighs to sing,
And all things with so sweet a sadness move,
As made my heart at once both grieve and love.

O fairer than aught else
  The world can show, leave off in time to grieve.
Enough, enough your joyful looks excels;
  Tears kills the heart, believe.
O! strive not to be excellent in woe,
Which only breeds your beauty's overthrow.

Anonymous

157

Clear or cloudy, sweet as April showering,
  Smooth or frowning, so is her face to me,
Pleas'd or smiling, like mild May all flowering,
  When skies blue silk, and meadows carpets be;
Her speeches, notes of that night bird that singeth,
Who, though all sweet, yet jarring notes out-ringeth.

Her grace like June, when earth and trees be trimmed
  In best attire of complete beauty's height;
Her love again like summer's days be-dimmed
  With little clouds of doubtful constant faith;
Her trust, her doubt, like rain and heat in skies
Gently thund'ring, she lightning to mine eyes.

Sweet summer-spring that breatheth life and growing
  In weeds as well as into herbs and flowers,
And seeds of service, divers sorts in sowing,
  Some haply seeming, and some being, yours;
Rain on your herbs and flowers that truly serve,
And let your weeds lack dew, and duly sterve.

Anonymous

158

Thule, the period of cosmography,
  Doth vaunt of Hecla, whose sulphureous fire
Doth melt the frozen clime and thaw the sky;
  Trinacrian Etna's flames ascend not higher:
These things seem wondrous, yet more wondrous I,
Whose heart with fear doth freeze, with love doth fry.

The Andalusian merchant that returns
  Laden with cochineal and china dishes,
Reports in Spain how strangely Fogo burns
  Amidst an ocean full of flying fishes:
These things seem wondrous, yet more wondrous I,
Whose heart with fear doth freeze, with love doth fry.

Anonymous

159

Love wing'd my hopes and taught me how to fly
Far from base earth, but not to mount too high.
          For true pleasure
          Lives in measure,
        Which, if men forsake,
Blinded they into folly run, and grief for pleasure take.

But my vain hopes, proud of their new-taught flight,
Enamour'd, sought to woo the sun's fair light,

Whose rich brightness
Moved their lightness
To aspire so high,
That, all scorch'd and consum'd with fire, now drown'd in woe they lie.

And none but Love their woeful hap did rue,
For love did know that their desires were true.
Though Fate frowned,
And now drowned
They in sorrow dwell,
It was the purest light of heaven for whose fair love they fell.

Anonymous

160

Follow your saint, follow with accents sweet;
Haste you, sad notes, fall at her flying feet.
There wrapp'd in cloud of sorrow, pity move,
And tell the ravisher of my soul I perish for her love.
But if she scorns my never-ceasing pain,
Then burst with sighing in her sight, and ne'er return again.

All that I sung still to her praise did tend.
Still she was first, still she my songs did end.
Yet she my love and music both doth fly,
The music that her echo is, and beauty's sympathy.
Then let my notes pursue her scornful flight;
It sha l suffice that they were breath'd, and died for her delight.

Thomas Campion

161

My sweetest Lesbia, let us live and love;
And, though the sager sort our deeds reprove,
Let us not weigh them. Heaven's great lamps do dive
Into their west, and straight again revive.
But soon as once set is our little light,
Then must we sleep one ever-during night.

If all would lead their lives in love like me,
Then bloody swords and armour should not be;
No drum nor trumpet peaceful sleeps should move,
Unless alarm came from the camp of Love.
But fools do live and waste their little light,
And seek with pain their ever-during night.

When timely death my life and fortune ends,
Let not my hearse be vex'd with mourning friends
But let all lovers, rich in triumph, come
And with sweet pastimes grace my happy tomb.
And, Lesbia, close up thou my little light,
And crown with love my ever-during night.

Thomas Campion

162

I care not for these ladies that must be wooed and prayed:
Give me kind Amaryllis, the wanton country maid.
Nature Art disdaineth; her beauty is her own.
Her when we court and kiss, she cries: 'Forsooth, let go!'
But when we come where comfort is, she never will say no.

If I love Amaryllis, she gives me fruit and flowers;
But if we love these ladies, we must give golden showers.
Give them gold that sell love, give me the nut-brown lass,
Who when we court and kiss, she cries: 'Forsooth, let go!'
But when we come where comfort is, she never will say no.

These ladies must have pillows and beds by strangers wrough
Give me a bower of willows, of moss and leaves unbought,
And fresh Amaryllis with milk and honey fed,
Who when we court and kiss, she cries: 'Forsooth, let go!'
But when we come where comfort is, she never will say no.

Thomas Campion

163

Turn back, you wanton flyer,
And answer my desire
  With mutual greeting,
Yet bend a little nearer,
True beauty still shines clearer
  In closer meeting.
Hearts with hearts delighted
Should strive to be united
Either other's arms with arms enchaining;
    Hearts with a thought,
Rosy lips with a kiss still entertaining.

What harvest half so sweet is
As still to reap the kisses
  Grown ripe in sowing;
And straight to be receiver
Of that which thou art giver,
  Rich in bestowing?
There's no strict observing
Of times' or seasons' swerving,
There is ever one fresh spring abiding;
  Then what we sow,
With our lips let us reap, love's gains dividing.

Thomas Campion

164

Thou art not fair, for all thy red and white,
  For all those rosy ornaments in thee.
Thou art not sweet, though made of mere delight,
  Nor fair nor sweet, unless thou pity me.
I will not soothe thy fancies. Thou shalt prove
That beauty is no beauty without love.

Yet love not me, nor seek thou to allure
  My thoughts with beauty, were it more divine;
Thy smiles and kisses I cannot endure,
  I'll not be wrapp'd up in those arms of thine.
Now show it, if thou be a woman right,
Embrace and kiss and love me in despite.

Thomas Campion

165

The man of life upright,
  Whose guiltless heart is free
From all dishonest deeds
  Or thought of vanity:

The man whose silent days
  In harmless joys are spent,
Whom hopes cannot delude,
  Nor sorrow discontent:

That man needs neither towers
  Nor armour for defence,
Nor secret vaults to fly
  From thunder's violence.

He only can behold
  With unaffrighted eyes
The horrors of the deep
  And terrors of the skies.

Thus scorning all the cares
  That fate or fortune brings,
He makes the heaven his book,
  His wisdom heavenly things,

Good thoughts his only friends,
His wealth a well-spent age,
The earth his sober inn
And quiet pilgrimage.

Thomas Campion

166

When thou must home to shades of underground,
And there arrived, a new admired guest,
The beauteous spirits do engirt thee round,
White Iope, blithe Helen and the rest,
To hear the stories of thy finish'd love
From that smooth tongue, whose music hell can move:

Then wilt thou speak of banqueting delights,
Of masks and revels which sweet youth did make,
Of tourneys and great challenges of knights,
And all these triumphs for thy beauty's sake.
When thou hast told these honours done to thee,
Then tell, Oh, tell how thou didst murder me.

Thomas Campion

167

Weep you no more, sad fountains;
What need you flow so fast?
Look how the snowy mountains
Heaven's sun doth gently waste.
But my sun's heavenly eyes
View not your weeping,
That now lies sleeping
Softly, now softly lies
Sleeping.

Sleep is a reconciling,
A rest that peace begets.
Doth not the sun rise smiling
When fair at even he sets?

Rest you, then rest, sad eyes,
  Melt not in weeping,
  While she lies sleeping
Softly, now softly lies
    Sleeping.

Anonymous

168

What poor astronomers are they
  Take women's eyes for stars,
And set their thoughts in battle 'ray
  To fight such idle wars;
When in the end they shall approve
'Tis but a jest drawn out of love.

And love itself is but a jest
  Devis'd by idle heads,
To catch young fancies in the nest
  And lay them in fools' beds;
That being hatch'd in beauty's eyes
They may be flidge ere they be wise.

But yet it is a sport to see
  How wit will run on wheels,
While will cannot persuaded be
  With that which reason feels;
That women's eyes and stars are odd,
And Love is but a feigned god.

But such as will run mad with will,
  I cannot clear their sight,
But leave them to their study still
  To look where is no light;
Till time too late we make them try
They study false astronomy.

Anonymous

169

Fain would I change that note
  To which fond love hath charm'd me;
Long, long to sing by rote,
  Fancying that that harm'd me.
Yet when this thought doth come
'Love is the perfect sum
  Of all delight,'
I have no other choice
Either for pen or voice
  To sing or write.

O Love, they wrong thee much
  That say thy sweet is bitter,
When thy ripe fruit is such
  As nothing can be sweeter.
Fair house of joy and bliss,
Where truest pleasure is,
  I do adore thee;
I know thee what thou art,
I serve thee with my heart
  And fall before thee.

Anonymous

170

There is a lady sweet and kind,
Was never face so pleased my mind;
I did but see her passing by,
And yet I love her till I die.

Her gesture, motion, and her smiles,
Her wit, her voice, my heart beguiles,
Beguiles my heart, I know not why,
And yet I love her till I die.

Her free behaviour, winning looks,
Will make a lawyer burn his books;
I touch'd her not, alas! not I,
And yet I love her till I die.

Had I her fast betwixt mine arms,
Judge you that think such sports were harms
Were't any harm? no, no, fie, fie,
For I will love her till I die.

Should I remain confined there
So long as Phoebus in his sphere,
I to request, she to deny,
Yet would I love her till I die.

Cupid is wingèd and doth range,
Her country so my love doth change:
But change she earth, or change she sky,
Yet will I love her till I die.

Anonymous

171

Do not, O do not prize thy beauty at too high a rate;
Love to be loved whilst thou art lovely, lest thou love too late
Frowns print wrinkles in thy brows,
At which spiteful age doth smile,
Women in their froward vows
Glorying to beguile.

Wert thou the only world's-admired, thou canst love but one
And many have before been lov'd, thou art not lov'd alone.
Couldst thou speak with heavenly grace,
Sappho might with thee compare;
Blush the roses in thy face,
Rosamund was as fair.

'ride is the canker that consumeth beauty in her prime.
'hey that delight in long debating feel the curse of time.
All things with the time do change,
That will not the time obey.
Some e'en to themselves seem strange
Thorough their own delay. *Anonymous*

172

Ha, ha! Ha, ha! This world doth pass
Most merrily, I'll be sworn,
For many an honest Indian ass
Goes for a unicorn.
Fara diddle dyno,
This is idle fyno.

Tee-hee! Tee-hee! O sweet delight!
He tickles this age that can
Call Tullia's ape a marmosyte
And Leda's goose a swan.
Fara diddle dyno,
This is idle fyno.

So, so! so, so! Fine English days!
For false play is no reproach,
For he that doth the coachman praise
May safely use the coach.
Fara diddle dyno,
This is idle fyno. *Anonymous*

173

The sea hath many thousand sands,
The sun has notes as many,
Thy sky is full of stars, and love
As full of woes as any.
Believe me, that do know the elf,
And make no trial by thyself.

It is in truth a pretty toy
  For babes to play withal.
But oh, the honeys of our youth
  Are oft our age's gall.
Self-proof in time will make thee know
He was a prophet told thee so.

A prophet that Cassandra-like
  Tells truth without belief,
For headstrong youth will run his race
  Although his goal be grief.
Love's martyr, when his heat is past,
Proves Care's confessor at the last.

Anonymous

174

Think'st thou to seduce me then with words that have no
  meaning?
Parrots so can learn to prate, our speech by pieces gleaning:
Nurses teach their children so about the time of weaning.

Learn to speak first, then to woo: to wooing much pertaineth
He that courts us, wanting art, soon falters when he feigneth
Looks asquint on his discourse and smiles when he complaineth

Skilful anglers hide their hooks, fit baits for every season,
But with crooked pins fish thou, as babes do that want reason
Gudgeons only can be caught with such poor tricks of treason

Ruth forgive me, if I erred from human heart's compassion,
When I laugh'd sometimes too much to see thy foolish fashion
But, alas, who less could do, that found so good occasion?

Thomas Campion

175

Never weather-beaten sail more willing bent to shore,
Never tired pilgrims limbs affected slumber more,
Than my wearied spright now longs to fly out of my troubled
breast.
O! come quickly, sweetest Lord, and take my soul to rest.

Ever blooming are the joys of Heaven's high Paradise.
Cold age deafs not there our ears, nor vapour dims our eyes;
Glory there the sun outshines, whose beams the blessed only
see.
O! come quickly, glorious Lord, and raise my sprite to thee.

Thomas Campion

176

Come, you pretty false-eyed wanton,
Leave your crafty smiling.
Think you to escape me now
With slippery words beguiling?
No, you mock'd me th'other day,
When you got loose, you fled away.
But since I have caught you now,
I'll clip your wings for flying;
Smothering kisses fast I'll heap,
And keep you so from crying.

Sooner may you count the stars,
And number hail down-pouring,
Tell the osiers of the Thames,
Or Goodwin Sands devouring,
Than the thick-shower'd kisses here,
Which now thy tired lips must bear.
Such a harvest never was,
So rich and full of pleasure;
But 'tis spent as soon as reaped,
So trustless is love's treasure.

Would it were dumb midnight now,
  When all the world lies sleeping.
Would this place some desert were,
  Which no man hath in keeping.
My desires should then be safe,
And when you cried, then would I laugh.
But if aught might breed offence,
  Love only should be blamed.
I would live your servant still,
  And you my saint unnamed.

Thomas Campion

177

  Kind are her answers,
But her performance keeps no day;
  Breaks time, as dancers
From their own music when they stray.
  All her free favours
And smooth words wing my hopes in vain.
  O! did ever voice so sweet but only feign?
Can true love yield such delay,
  Converting joy to pain?

  Lost is our freedom
When we submit to women so.
  Why do we need them
When in their best they work our woe?
  There is no wisdom
Can alter ends by Fate prefix'd.
  O! why is the good of man with evil mix'd?
Never were days yet call'd two,
  But one night went betwixt.

Thomas Campion

178

Now winter nights enlarge
  The number of their hours,
And clouds their storms discharge
  Upon the airy towers.
Let now the chimneys blaze,
  And cups o'erflow with wine;
Let well-tun'd words amaze
  With harmony divine.
  Now yellow waxen lights
    Shall wait on honey Love,
While youthful revels, masks, and courtly sights
    Sleep's leaden spells remove.

  This time doth well dispense
    With lovers' long discourse.
  Much speech hath some defence,
    Though beauty no remorse.
  All do not all things well:
    Some measures comely tread,
  Some knotted riddles tell,
    Some poems smoothly read.
  The Summer hath his joys,
    And Winter his delights.
Though Love and all his pleasures are but toys,
    They shorten tedious nights.

Thomas Campion

179

Thrice toss these oaken ashes in the air;
Thrice sit thou mute in this enchanted chair;
Then thrice three times tie up this true love's knot,
And murmur soft: 'She will, or she will not.'

Go burn these poisonous weeds in yon blue fire,
These screech-owl's feathers and this prickling briar,
This cypress gathered at a dead man's grave,
That all thy fears and cares an end may have.

Then come, you fairies, dance with me a round;
Melt her hard heart with your melodious sound.
In vain are all the charms I can devise;
She hath an art to break them with her eyes.

Thomas Campion

180

Turn all thy thoughts to eyes,
Turn all thy hairs to ears,
Change all thy friends to spies,
And all thy joys to fears:
True love will yet be free
In spite of jealousy.

Turn darkness into day,
Conjectures into truth,
Believe what th'envious say,
Let age interpret youth:
True love will yet be free,
In spite of jealousy.

Wrest every word and look,
Rack ev'ry hidden thought,
Or fish with golden hook;
True love cannot be caught.
For that will still be free
In spite of jealousy.

Thomas Campion

POEMS FROM VARIOUS SOURCES

181

Of all the birds that I do know,
  Philip, my sparrow, hath no peer:
For sit she high or lie she low,
  Be she far off, or be she near,
There is no bird so fair, so fine,
Nor yet so fresh as this of mine.

Come in a morning merrily,
  When Philip hath been lately fed,
Or in an evening soberly,
  When Philip list to go to bed:
It is a heaven to hear my Phippe,
How she can chirp with cherry lip.

She never wanders far abroad,
  But is at hand when I do call;
If I command, she lays on load
  With lips, with teeth, with tongue and an.
She chants, she chirps, she makes such cheer,
That I believe she hath no peer.

And yet besides all this good sport,
  My Philip can both sing and dance;
With new-found toys of sundry sort
  My Philip can both prick and prance:
As if you say but 'fend cut, Phippe,'
Lord! how the peat will turn and skip.

Her feathers are so fresh of hue,
  And so well proyned every day:
She lacks no oil, I warrant you,
  To trim her tail both trick and gay.
And though her mouth be somewhat wide,
Her tongue is sweet and short beside.

And for the rest I dare compare,
  She is both tender, sweet and soft;
She never lacketh dainty fare,
  But is well fed, and feedeth oft:
For if my Phippe have lust to eate,
I warrant you Phippe lacks no meat.

And then if that her meat be good,
  And such as like do love alway,
She will lay lips thereon, by the rood!
  And see that none be cast away:
For when she once hath felt a fit,
Philip will cry still 'Yit, yit, yit.'

And, to tell truth, he were to blame,
  Which had so fine a bird as she,
To make him all this goodly game
  Without suspect or jealousy:
He were a churl and knew no good
Would see her faint for lack of food.

Wherefore I sing and ever shall
  To praise as I have often proved:
There is no bird amongst them all
  So worthy for to be beloved.
Let other praise what bird they will,
Sweet Philip shall be my bird still.

George Gascoigne

182

Ye dainty nymphs, that in this blessed brook
  Do bathe your breast,
Forsake your watery bowers, and hither look,
  At my request;
And eke you virgins, that on Parnasse dwell,
Whence floweth Helicon the learned well,
  Help me to blaze
  Her worthy praise,
Which in her sex doth all excel.

Of fair Elisa be your silver song,
  That blessed wight;
The flower of virgins, may she flourish long,
  In princely plight.
For she is Syrinx' daughter without spot,
Which Pan the shepherds' God of her begot:
  So sprang her grace
  Of heavenly race,
No mortal blemish may her blot.

See, where she sits upon the grassy green,
  (O seemly sight)
Yclad in scarlet like a maiden Queen,
  And ermines white.
Upon her head a cremosin coronet
With damask roses and daffodillies set:
  Bay-leaves between,
  And primroses green
Embellish the sweet violet.

Tell me, have ye seen her angelic face,
  Like Phoebe fair?
Her heavenly haviour, her princely grace,
  Can you well compare?

The red rose medled with the white yfere
In either cheek depeincten lively cheer.
  Her modest eye,
  Her majesty,
Where have you seen the like, but there?

I saw Phoebus thrust out his golden head,
  Upon her to gaze:
But when he saw, how broad her beams did spread,
  It did him amaze.
He blushed to see another sun below,
Ne durst again his fiery face outshow:
  Let him, if he dare,
  His brightness compare
With hers, to have the overthrow.

Shew thyself, Cynthia, with thy silver rays,
  And be not abashed;
When she the beams of her beauty displays,
  O how art thou dashed?
But I will not match her with Latona's seed;
Such folly great sorrow to Niobe did breed.
  Now she is a stone,
  And makes daily moan,
Warning all other to take heed.

Pan may be proud, that ever he begot
  Such a bellibone,
And Syrinx rejoice, that ever was her lot
  To bear such an one.
Soon as my younglings cryen for the dam,
To her will I offer a milkwhite lamb.
  She is my goddess plain,
  And I her shepherd's swain,
Albeit forswonk and forswat I am.

I see Calliope speed her to the place,
  Where my goddess shines;
And after her the other Muses trace,
  With their violins.
Been they not bay branches, which they do bear,
All for Elisa in her hand to wear?
  So sweetly they play,
  And sing all the way,
That it a heaven is to hear.

Lo, how finely the Graces can it foot
  To the instrument;
They dancen deftly, and singen soote,
  In their merriment.
Wants not a fourth Grace, to make the dance even?
Let that room to my lady be yeven:
  She shall be a Grace,
  To fill the fourth place,
And reign with the rest in heaven.

And whither runs this bevy of ladies bright,
  Ranged in a row?
They been all ladies of the lake behight,
  That unto her go.
Chloris, that is the chiefest nymph of all,
Of olive branches bears a coronal:
  Olives been for peace,
  When wars do surcease;
Such for a princess been principal.

Ye shepherds' daughters, that dwell on the green,
  Hie you there apace;
Let none come there, but that virgins been,
  To adorn her grace.

And when you come, whereas she is in place,
See, that your rudeness do not you disgrace:
Bind your fillets fast,
And gird in your waist,
For more fineness, with a tawdry lace.

Bring hither the pink and purple columbine,
With gillyflowers;
Bring coronations, and sops in wine,
Worn of paramours.
Strew me the ground with daffadowndillies,
And cowslips, and kingcups, and loved lilies:
The pretty paunce,
And the chevisaunce,
Shall match with the fair flower delice.

Now rise up Elisa, decked as thou art,
In royal array;
And now ye dainty damsels may depart
Each one her way,
I fear, I have troubled your troops too long;
Let Dame Elisa thank you for her song.
And if you come hither,
When damsons I gather,
I will part them all you among.

Edmund Spenser

183

Time wasteth years, and months, and days, and hours,
Time doth consume fame, honour, wit, and strength,
Time kills the greenest herbs and sweetest flowers,
Time wears out youth and beauty's looks at length,
Time doth convey to ground both foe and friend,
Ane each thing else but love, which hath no end.

Time maketh every tree to die and rot,
  Time turneth oft our pleasures into pain,
Time causeth wars and wrongs to be forgot,
  Time clears the sky, which first hung full of rain,
    Time makes an end of all humane desire,
    But only this, which sets my heart on fire.

Time turneth into nought each princely state,
  The brings a flood from new resolved snow,
Time calms the sea where tempest was of late,
  Time eats whate'er the moon can see below;
    And yet no time prevails in my behove,
    Nor any time can make me cease to love.

Thomas Watson

184

My prime of youth is but a frost of cares,
  My feast of joy is but a dish of pain,
My crop of corn is but a field of tares,
  And all my good is but vain hope of gain;
    The day is past, and yet I saw no sun,
    And now I live, and now my life is done.

My tale was heard and yet it was not told,
  My fruit is fallen and yet my leaves are green,
My youth is spent and yet I am not old,
  I saw the world and yet I was not seen;
    My thread is cut and yet it is not spun,
    And now I live, and now my life is done.

I sought my death and found it in my womb,
  I look'd for life and saw it was a shade,
I trod the earth and knew it was my tomb,
  And now I die, and now I was but made;
    My glass is full, and now my glass is run,
    And now I live, and now my life is done.

Chidiock Tichborne

185

The earth, late chok'd with showers,
  Is now array'd in green;
Her bosom springs with flowers,
  The air dissolves her teen:
The heavens laugh at her glory,
Yet bide I sad and sorry.

The woods are deck'd with leaves,
  And trees are clothed gay;
And Flora, crown'd with sheaves,
  With oaken boughs doth play:
Where I am clad in black,
The token of my wrack.

The birds upon the trees
  Do sing with pleasant voices,
And chant in their degrees
  Their loves and lucky choices:
When I, whilst they are singing,
With sighs mine arms am wringing.

The thrushes seek the shade,
  And I my fatal grave;
Their flight to heaven is made,
  My walk on earth I have:
They free, I thrall; they jolly,
I sad and pensive wholly.

Thomas Lodge

186

His golden locks time hath to silver turn'd;
  O time too swift, O swiftness never ceasing!
His youth 'gainst time and age hath ever spurn'd,
  But spurn'd in vain; youth waneth by increasing:

Beauty, strength, youth, are flowers but fading seen;
Duty, faith, love, are roots, and ever green.

His helmet now shall make a hive for bees;
  And, lovers' sonnets turned to holy psalms,
A man-at-arms must now serve on his knees,
  And feed on prayers, which are age's alms:
But though from court to cottage he depart,
His saint is sure of his unspotted heart.

And when he saddest sits in homely cell,
  He'll teach his swains this carol for a song:
'Blest be the hearts that wish my sovereign well,
  Curst be the souls that think her any wrong.'
Goddess, allow this aged man his right,
To be your beadsman now, that was your knight.

George Peele

187

Only joy, now here you are,
Fit to hear and ease my care;
Let my whispering voice obtain
Sweet reward for sharpest pain;
Take me to thee, and thee to me.
No, no, no, no, my dear, let be.

Night hath closed all in her cloak,
Twinkling stars love-thoughts provoke,
Danger hence good care doth keep,
Jealousy itself doth sleep;
Take me to thee, and thee to me.
No, no, no, no, my dear, let be.

Better place no wit can find,
Cupid's yoke to loose or bind;
These sweet flowers on fine bed too
Us in their best language woo;
Take me to thee, and thee to me.
No, no, no, no, my dear, let be.

This small light the moon bestows
Serves thy beams but to disclose;
So to raise my hap more high,
Fear not, else none can us spy;
Take me to thee, and thee to me.
No, no, no, no, my dear, let be.

That you heard was but a mouse,
Dumb sleep holdeth all the house;
Yet asleep, methinks, they say,
Young folks, take time while you may;
Take me to thee, and thee to me.
No, no, no, no, my dear, let be.

Niggard Time threats, if we miss
This large offer of our bliss,
Long stay ere he grant the same;
Sweet, then, while each thing doth frame,
Take me to thee, and thee to me.
No, no, no, no, my dear, let be.

Your fair mother is a-bed,
Candles out and curtains spread;
She thinks you do letters write;
Write, but let me first indite:
Take me to thee, and thee to me.
No, no, no, no, my dear, let be.

Sweet, alas, why strive you thus?
Concord better fitteth us;
Leave to Mars the force of hands,
Your power in your beauty stands;
Take thee to me, and me to thee.
No, no, no, no, my dear, let be.

Woe to me! and do you swear
Me to hate, but I forbear?
Cursed be my destines all,
That brought me so high to fall!
Soon with my death I will please thee.
No, no, no, no, my dear, let be.

Sir Philip Sidney

188

Hark, all you ladies that do sleep!
  The fairy queen Proserpina
Bids you awake, and pity them that weep.
  You may do in the dark
    What the day doth forbid.
  Fear not the dogs that bark;
    Night will have all hid.

But if you let your lovers moan,
  The fairy queen Proserpina
Will send abroad her fairies every one,
  That shall pinch black and blue
    Your white hands and fair arms,
  That did not kindly rue
    Your paramours' harms.

In myrtle arbours on the downs,
  The fair queen Proserpina
This night, by moonshine, leading merry rounds,

Holds a watch with sweet Love,
Down the dale, up the hill;
No plaints nor griefs may move
Their holy vigil.

All you that will hold watch with Love,
The fairy queen Proserpina
Will make you fairer than Dione's dove.
Roses red, lilies white,
And the clear damask hue,
Shall on your cheeks alight.
Love will adorn you.

All you that love, or lov'd before,
The fairy queen Proserpina
Bids you increase that loving humour more.
They that have not yet fed
On delights amorous,
She vows that they shall lead
Apes in Avernus.

Thomas Campion

189

What if a day, or a month, or a year
Crown thy desire with a thousand sweet contentings?
Cannot the chance of a night or an hour
Cross thy delight with as many sad tormentings?
Fortune, honour, beauty, youth,
Are but blossoms dying;
Wanton pleasures, doting love,
Are but shadows flying.
All our joys,
Are but toys,

Idle thoughts deceiving.
None have power
Of an hour
In their lives' bereaving.

Earth's but a point to the world; and a man
Is but a point to the earth's compared centre;
Shall then a point in a point be so vain
As to triumph in a silly point's adventure?
All is hazard that we have,
Here is no abiding;
Days of pleasure are but streams
Through fair meadows gliding.
Weal or woe,
Time doth go;
In time's no returning.
Secret fates
Guide our states
Both in mirth and mourning.

Anonymous

190

My Phillis hath the morning sun
At first to look upon her;
And Phillis hath morn-waking birds
Her risings for to honour.
My Phillis hath prime-feather'd flowers
That smiles when she treads on them;
And Phillis hath a gallant flock
That leaps since she doth own them.
But Phillis hath so hard a heart—
Alas that she should have it!
As yields no mercy to desert,
Nor grace to those that crave it.

Sweet sun, when thou look'st on,
Pray her regard my moan;
Sweet birds, when you sing to her,
To yield some pity, woo her;
Sweet flowers, whenas she treads on,
Tell her, her beauty deads one:
And if in life her love she nill agree me,
Pray her, before I die she will come see me.

Thomas Lodge

191

A Child My Choice

Let folly praise that fancy loves, I praise and love that child,
Whose heart no thought, whose tongue no word, whose hand no deed defiled.
I praise him most, I love him best, all praise and love is his:
While him I love, in him I live, and cannot live amiss.

Love's sweetest mark, laud's highest theme, man's most desired light:
To love him, life; to leave him, death; to live in him, delight.
He mine, by gift; I his, by debt; thus each to other's due:
First friend he was; best friend he is; all times will try him true.

Alas! he weeps, he sighs, he pants; yet do his angels sing:
Out of his tears, his sighs and throbs doth bud a joyful spring.
Almighty Babe, whose tender arms can force all foes to fly,
Correct my faults, protect my life, direct me when I die.

Robert Southwell

192

As I in hoary winter's night stood shivering in the snow,
Surpris'd I was with sudden heat which made my heart to glow;
And lifting up a fearful eye to view what fire was near,
A pretty Babe all burning bright did in the air appear;

Vho, scorched with excessive heat, such floods of tears did
shed,
s though his floods should quench his flames which with his
tears were fed.
Alas!' quoth he, 'but newly born in fiery heats I fry,
et none approach to warm their hearts or feel my fire but I.
Iy faultless breast the furnace is, the fuel wounding thorns;
ove is the fire, and sighs the smoke, the ashes shame and
scorns;
he fuel justice layeth on, and mercy blows the coals;
he metal in this furnace wrought are men's defiled souls:
or which, as now on fire I am to work them to their good,
o will I melt into a bath to wash them in my blood.'
Vith this he vanish'd out of sight and swiftly shrunk away,
nd straight I called unto mind that it was Christmas day.

Robert Southwell

193

Come to your heaven, you heavenly choirs!
Earth hath the heaven of your desires;
Remove your dwelling to your God,
A stall is now his best abode;
Sith men their homage do deny,
Come, angels, all their fault supply.

His chilling cold doth heat require,
Come, seraphins, in lieu of fire;
This little ark no cover hath,
Let cherubs' wings his body swathe;
Come, Raphael, this Babe must eat,
Provide our little Toby meat.

Let Gabriel be now his groom,
That first took up his earthly room;

Let Michael stand in his defence,
Whom love hath link'd to feeble sense;
Let graces rock when he doth cry,
And angels sing his lullaby.

The same you saw in heavenly seat,
Is he that now sucks Mary's teat;
Agnize your King a mortal wight,
His borrow'd weed lets not your sight;
Come, kiss the manger where he lies,
That is your bliss above the skies.

This little Babe, so few days old,
Is come to rifle Satan's fold;
All hell doth at his presence quake,
Though he himself for cold do shake;
For in this weak unarmed wise
The gates of hell he will surprise.

With tears he fights and wins the field,
His naked breast stands for a shield;
His battering shot are babish cries,
His arrows looks of weeping eyes.
His martial ensigns cold and need,
And feeble flesh his warrior's steed.

His camp is pitched in a stall,
His bulwark but a broken wall;
The crib his trench, hay-stalks his stakes,
Of shepherds he his muster makes;
And thus, as sure his foe to wound,
The angels' trumps alarum sound.

My soul, with Christ join thou in fight;
Stick to the tents that he hath pight;

Within his crib is surest ward,
This little Babe will be thy guard;
If thou wilt foil thy foes with joy,
Then flit not from this heavenly boy.

Robert Southwell

194

The nightingale, as soon as April bringeth
  Unto her rested sense a perfect waking,
While late bare earth, proud of new clothing, springeth,
  Sings out her woes, a thorn her song-book making;
  And mournfully bewailing,
Her throat in tunes expresseth
What grief her breast oppresseth
  For Tereus' force on her chaste will prevailing.
O Philomela fair! Oh, take some gladness
That here is juster cause of plaintful sadness.
    Thine earth now springs, mine fadeth;
    Thy thorn without, my thorn my heart invadeth.

Alas, she hath no other cause of anguish
  But Tereus' love, on her by strong hand wroken,
Wherein she suffering, all her spirits languish;
  Full womanlike complains her will was broken.
  But I, who daily craving,
Cannot have to content me,
Have more cause to lament me,
  Since wanting is more woe than too much having.
O Philomela fair! Oh take some gladness
That here is juster cause of plaintful sadness.
    Thine earth now springs, mine fadeth;
    Thy thorn without, my thorn my heart invadeth.

Sir Philip Sidney

195

Ring out your bells, let mourning shows be spread;
For Love is dead.
  All Love is dead, infected
With plague of deep disdain;
  Worth, as nought worth, rejected,
And Faith fair scorn doth gain.
  From so ungrateful fancy,
  From such a female franzy,
    From them that use men thus,
    Good Lord, deliver us!

Weep, neighbours, weep! do you not hear it said
That Love is dead?
  His death-bed, peacock's folly;
His winding-sheet is shame;
  His will, false-seeming holy;
His sole executor, blame.
  From so ungrateful fancy,
  From such a female franzy,
    From them that use men thus,
    Good Lord, deliver us!

Let dirge be sung and trentals rightly read,
For Love is dead.
  Sir Wrong his tomb ordaineth,
My mistress' marble-heart,
  Which epitaph containeth,
'Her eyes were once his dart.'
  From so ungrateful fancy,
  From such a female franzy,
    From them that use men thus,
    Good Lord, deliver us!

Alas! I lie, rage hath this error bred;
Love is not dead.
Love is not dead, but sleepeth
In her unmatched mind,
Where she his counsel keepeth,
Till due desert she find.
Therefore from so vile fancy,
To call such wit a franzy,
Who Love can temper thus,
Good Lord, deliver us!

Sir Philip Sidney

196

As it fell upon a day,
In the merry month of May,
Sitting in a pleasant shade,
Which a grove of myrtles made,
Beasts did leap, and birds did sing,
Trees did grow, and plants did spring;
Every thing did banish moan
Save the nightingale alone.
She, poor bird, as all forlorn,
Lean'd her breast uptil a thorn,
And there sung the dolefull'st ditty,
That to hear it was great pity.
Fie, fie, fie, now would she cry;
Tereu, tereu, by and by:
That to hear her so complain
Scarce I could from tears refrain:
For her griefs so lively shown
Made me think upon mine own.
Ah, thought I, thou mourn'st in vain,
None takes pity on thy pain:
Senseless trees, they cannot hear thee,
Ruthless beasts, they will not cheer thee;

King Pandion, he is dead,
All thy friends are lapp'd in lead;
All thy fellow birds do sing,
Careless of thy sorrowing:
Even so, poor bird, like thee,
None alive will pity me.

Richard Barnfield

197

Every night from even till morn,
Love's chorister amid the thorn
Is now so sweet a singer;
So sweet, as for her song I scorn
Apollo's voice and finger.

But nightingale, sith you delight
Ever to watch the starry night,
Tell all the stars of heaven,
Heaven never had a star so bright,
As now to earth is given.

Royal Astraea makes our day
Eternal with her beams, nor may
Gross darkness overcome her.
I now perceive why some do write,
No country hath so short a night,
As England hath in summer.

Sir John Davies

198

'As you came from the holy land
Of Walsinghame,
Met you not with my true love
By the way as you came?'

'How shall I know your true love,
  That have met many one
As I went to the holy land,
  That have come, that have gone?'

'She is neither white nor brown,
  But as the heavens fair,
There is none hath a form so divine
  In the earth or the air.'

'Such an one did I meet, good Sir,
  Such an angelic face,
Who like a queen, like a nymph did appear
  By her gait, by her grace.'

'She hath left me here all alone,
  All alone as unknown,
Who sometimes did me lead with herself,
  And me lov'd as her own.'

'What's the cause that she leaves you alone
  And a new way doth take,
Who loved you once as her own
  And her joy did you make?'

'I have lov'd her all my youth,
  But now old as you see,
Love likes not the falling fruit
  From the withered tree.

'Know that Love is a careless child,
  And forgets promise past;
He is blind, he is deaf when he list
  And in faith never fast,

'His desire is a dureless content
And a trustless joy;
He is won with a world of despair
And is lost with a toy.

'Of womenkind such indeed is the love
Or the word love abused,
Under which many childish desires
And conceits are excused.

'But love is a durable fire
In the mind ever burning;
Never sick, never old, never dead,
From itself never turning.'

Sir Walter Ralegh

199

Let the bird of loudest lay,
On the sole Arabian tree,
Herald sad and trumpet be,
To whose sound chaste wings obey.

But thou shrieking harbinger,
Foul precurrer of the fiend,
Augur of the fever's end,
To this troop come thou not near.

From this session interdict
Every fowl of tyrant wing,
Save the eagle, feather'd king;
Keep the obsequy so strict.

Let the priest in surplice white
That defunctive music can,
Be the death-divining swan,
Lest the requiem lack his right.

And thou treble-dated crow,
That thy sable gender mak'st
With the breath thou givest and tak'st,
'Mongst our mourners shalt thou go.

Here the anthem doth commence:
Love and constancy is dead;
Phoenix and the Turtle fled
In a mutual flame from hence.

So they loved, as love in twain
Had the essence but in one;
Two distincts, division none;
Number there in love was slain.

Hearts remote, yet not asunder;
Distance, and no space was seen
'Twixt the Turtle and his queen;
But in them it were a wonder.

So between them Love did shine,
That the Turtle saw his right
Flaming in the Phoenix' sight;
Either was the other's mine.

Property was thus appalled,
That the self was not the same;
Single nature's double name
Neither two nor one was called.

Reason, in itself confounded,
Saw division grow together,
To themselves yet either neither,
Simple were so well compounded:

That it cried, 'How true a twain
Seemeth this concordant one!
Love hath reason, Reason none,
If what parts can so remain.'

Whereupon it made this threne
To the Phoenix and the Dove,
Co-supremes and stars of Love,
As chorus to their tragic scene.

Threnos

Beauty, Truth, and Rarity,
Grace in all simplicity,
Here enclos'd in cinders lie.

Death is now the Phoenix' nest;
And the Turtle's loyal breast
To eternity doth rest.

Leaving no posterity:
'Twas not their infirmity,
It was married chastity.

Truth may seem, but cannot be;
Beauty brag, but 'tis not she;
Truth and Beauty buried be.

To this urn let those repair
That are either true or fair;
For these dead birds sigh a prayer.

William Shakespeare

200

Epitaph on S.P.
A Child of Queen Elizabeth's Chapel

Weep with me, all you that read
  This little story;
And know, for whom a tear you shed
  Death's self is sorry.
'Twas a child that so did thrive
  In grace and feature,
As Heaven and Nature seem'd to strive
  Which own'd the creature.
Years he number'd scarce thirteen,
  When Fates turn'd cruel;
Yet three fill'd zodiacs had he been
  The stage's jewel;
And did act, what now we moan,
  Old men so duly,
As sooth the Parcae thought him one,
  He play'd so truly.
So, by error, to his fate
  They all consented;
But, viewing him since—alas, too late!—
  They have repented;
And have sought, to give new birth,
  In baths to steep him;
But, being so much too good for earth,
  Heaven vows to keep him.

Ben Jonson

201

Give me my scallop-shell of Quiet,
My staff of Faith to walk upon,
My scrip of Joy, immortal diet.
My bottle of Salvation,

My gown of Glory, Hope's true gage,
And thus I'll take my pilgrimage.

Blood must be my body's balmer.
No other balm will there be given,
Whilst my soul like a white palmer
Travels to the land of heaven,
Over the silver mountains,
Where spring the nectar fountains;
And there I'll kiss
The bowl of bliss,
And drink my everlasting fill
On every milken hill.
My soul will be a-dry before,
But after it will thirst no more.

And by the happy blissful way
More peaceful pilgrims I shall see,
That have shook off their gowns of clay
And go apparell'd fresh like me.
I'll bring them first
To slake their thirst,
And then taste those nectar suckets,
At the clear wells
Where sweetness dwells,
Drawn up by saints in crystal buckets.
And when our bottles and all we
Are filled with immortality,
Then the holy paths we'll travel,
Strew'd with rubies thick as gravel,
Ceilings of diamonds, sapphire floors,
High walls of coral and pearl bowers.

From thence to heaven's bribeless hall
Where no corrupted voices brawl,

No conscience molten into gold,
Nor forg'd accusers bought and sold,
No cause deferr'd, nor vain-spent journey,
For there Christ is the King's Attorney,
Who pleads for all without degrees,
And he hath angels, but no fees.

When the grand twelve million jury
Of our sins and direful fury
'Gainst our souls black verdicts give,
Christ pleads his death, and then we live.
Be thou my speaker, taintless pleader,
Unblotted lawyer, true proceeder;
Thou movest salvation even for alms,
Not with a bribed lawyer's palms.

And this is my eternal plea
To him that made heaven, earth, and sea:
Seeing my flesh must die so soon,
And want a head to dine next noon,
Just at the stroke when my veins start and spread
Set on my soul an everlasting head.
Then am I ready, like a palmer fit,
To tread those blest paths which before I writ.

Sir Water Ralegh

202

SIREN

Come, worthy Greek! Ulysses, come;
  Possess these shores with me!
The winds and seas are troublesome
  And here we may be free.
Mere may we sit and view their toil
  That travail in the deep,
And joy the day in mirth the while
  And spend the night in sleep.

ULYSSES

Fair nymph, if fame or honour were
  To be attain'd with ease,
Then would I come and rest me there,
  And leave such toils as these.
But here it dwells, and here must I
  With danger seek it forth:
To spend the time luxuriously
  Becomes not men of worth.

SIREN

Ulysses, O! be not deceived
  With that unreal name;
This honour is a thing conceived
  And rests on others' fame;
Begotten only to molest
  Our peace, and to beguile
The best thing of our life, our rest,
  And give us up to toil.

ULYSSES

Delicious nymph, suppose there were
  Nor honour nor report,
Yet manliness would scorn to wear
  The time in idle sport;
For toil doth give a better touch
  To make us feel our joy,
And ease finds tediousness as much
  As labour yields annoy.

SIREN

Then pleasure likewise seems the shore,
  Whereto tends all your toil,
Which you forgo to make it more,
  And perish oft the while.

Who may disport them diversely
  Find never tedious day,
And ease may have variety,
  As well as action may.

ULYSSES

But natures of the noblest frame
  These toils and dangers please;
And they take comfort in the same
  As much as you in ease;
And with the thought of actions past
  Are recreated still;
When pleasure leaves a touch at last,
  To shew that it was ill.

SIREN

That doth opinion only cause,
  That's out of custom bred,
Which makes us many other laws,
  Than ever nature did.
No widows wail for our delights,
  Our sports are without blood;
The world we see by warlike wights
  Receives more hurt than good.

ULYSSES

But yet the state of things require
  These motions of unrest;
And these great spirits of high desire
  Seem born to turn them best;
To purge the mischiefs that increase
  And all good order mar,
For oft we see a wicked peace
  To be well chang'd for war.

SIREN

Well, well, Ulysses, then I see
I shall not have thee here;
And therefore I will come to thee
And take my fortunes there.
I must be won that cannot win,
Yet lost were I not won,
For beauty hath created bin
T'undo, or be undone.

Samuel Daniel

203

Near to the silver Trent
Sirena dwelleth:
She to whom Nature lent
All that excelleth:
By which the Muses late,
And the neat Graces,
Have for their greater state
Taken their places:
Twisting an anadem
Wherewith to crown her,

As it belonged to them
Most to renown her.
On thy bank,
In a rank,
Let the swans sing her,
And with their music
Along let them bring her.

Tagus and Pactolus
Are to thee debter,
Nor for their gold to us
Are they the better:
Henceforth of all the rest,
Be thou the river,

Which as the daintiest
  Puts them down ever,
For as my precious one
  O'er thee doth travel,
She to pearl paragon
  Turneth thy gravel.
    On thy bank, etc

Our mournful Philomel,
  That rarest tuner,
Henceforth in Aperil
  Shall wake the sooner.
And to her shall complain
  From the thick cover,
Redoubling every strain
  Over and over:
For when my love too long
  Her chamber keepeth,
As though it suffer'd wrong,
  The morning weepeth.
    On thy bank, etc.

Oft have I seen the sun
  To do her honour
Fix himself at his noon
  To look upon her,
And hath gilt every grove,
  Every hill near her,
With his flames from above
  Striving to cheer her;
And when she from his sight
  Hath herself turned,
He, as it had been night,
  In clouds hath mourned.
    On thy bank, etc.

The verdant meads are seen,
  When she doth view them,
In fresh and gallant green
  Straight to renew them;
And every little grass
  Broad itself spreadeth,
Proud that this bonny lass
  Upon it treadet
Nor flower is so sweet
  In this large cincture
But it upon her feet
  Leaveth some tincture.
    On thy bank, etc.

The fishes in the flood,
  When she doth angle,
For the hook strive a good
  Them to entangle;
And leaping on the land
  From the clear water,
Their scales upon the sand
  Lavishly scatter;
Therewith to pave the mould
  Whereon she passes,
So herself to behold,
  As in her glasses.
    On thy bank, etc.

When she looks out by night,
  The stars stand gazing,
Like comets to our sight
  Fearfully blazing,
As wond'ring at her eyes
  With their much brightness,

Which so amaze the skies,
  Dimming their lightness.
The raging tempests are calm
  When she speaketh,
Such most delightsome balm
  From her lips breaketh.
    On thy bank, etc.

In all our Brittany,
  There's not a fairer,
Nor can you fit any,
  Should you compare her.
Angels her eye-lids keep,
  All hearts surprising.
Which look whilst she doth sleep
  Like the sun's rising.
She alone of her kind
  Knoweth true measure,
And her unmatched mind
  Is heaven's treasure.
    On thy bank, etc.

Fair Dove and Darwen clear,
  Boast ye your beauties,
To Trent your mistress here
  Yet pay your duties:
My love was higher born
  Tow'rds the full fountains,
Yet she doth moorland scorn
  And the Peak mountains;
Nor would she none should dream
  Where she abideth,
Humble as is the stream
  Which by her slideth.
    On thy bank, etc.

Yet my poor rustic Muse
Nothing can move her,
Nor the means I can use,
Though her true lover:
Many a long winter's night
Have I wak'd for her,
Yet this my piteous plight
Nothing can stir her.
All thy sands, silver Trent,
Down to the Humber,
The sighs that I have spent
Never can number.
On thy bank, etc.

Michael Drayton

204

I, with whose colours Myra dress'd her head,
I, that ware posies of her own hand-making,
I, that mine own name in the chimneys read
By Myra finely wrought ere I was waking;
Must I look on, in hope time coming may
With change bring back my turn again to play?

I, that on Sunday at the church-stile found
A garland sweet, with truc-lovc knots in flowers,
Which I to wear about mine arm was bound,
That each of us might know that all was ours;
Must I now lead an idle life in wishes,
And follow Cupid for his loaves and fishes?

I, that did wear the ring her mother left,
I, for whose love she gloried to be blamed,
I, with whose eyes her eyes committed theft,
I, who did make her blush when I was named;
Must I lose ring, flowers, blush, theft, and go naked,
Watching with sighs, till dead love be awaked?

I, that, when drowsy Argus fell asleep,
Like jealousy o'erwatched with desire,
Was ever warned modesty to keep,
While her breath, speaking, kindled Nature's fire;
Must I look on a-cold, while others warm them?
Do Vulcan's brothers in such fine nets arm them?

Was it for this that I might Myra see
Washing the water, with her beauties, white?
Yet would she never write her love to me.
Thinks wit of change, while thoughts are in delight?
Mad girls must safely love, as they may leave;
No man can print a kiss; lines may deceive.

Fulke Greville, Lord Brooke

205

Take heed of loving me;
At least remember I forbade it thee;
Not that I shall repair my unthrifty waste
Of breath and blood, upon thy sighs and tears,
By being to thee then what to me thou wast;
But so great joy our life at once outwears.
Then, lest thy love by my death frustrate be,
If thou love me, take heed of loving me.

Take heed of hating me,
Or too much triumph in the victory;
Not that I shall be mine own officer,
And hate with hate again retaliate;
But thou wilt lose the style of conqueror,
If I, thy conquest, perish by thy hate.
Then, lest my being nothing lessen thee,
If thou hate me, take heed of hating me.

Yet, love and hate me too;
So these extremes shall neither's office do;
Love me, that I may die the gentler way;
Hate me, because thy love is too great for me;
Or let these two, themselves, not me, decay;
So shall I live thy stage, not triumph be.
Lest thou thy love and hate and me undo,
To let me live, oh, love and hate me too!

John Donne

206

If yet I have not all thy love,
Dear, I shall never have it all.
I cannot breathe one other sigh to move,
Nor can entreat one other tear to fall;
And all my treasure, which should purchase thee,
Sighs, tears, and oaths, and letters I have spent.
Yet no more can be due to me,
Than at the bargain made was meant:
If then thy gift of love was partial,
That some to me, some should to others fall,
Dear, I shall never have thee all.

Or if then thou gavest me all,
All was but all which thou hadst then;
But if in thy heart since, there be, or shall
New love created be by other men,
Which have their stocks entire, and can in tears,
In sighs, in oaths, and letters, outbid me,
This new love may beget new fears,
For this love was not vowed by thee.
And yet it was, thy gift being general;
The ground, thy heart is mine: what ever shall
Grow there, dear, I should have it all.

Yet I would not have all yet:
He that hath all can have no more;
And since my love doth every day admit
  New growth, thou shouldst have new rewards in store;
Thou canst not every day give me thy heart,
  If thou canst give it, then thou never gavest it:
Love's riddles are, that though thy heart depart,
  It stays at home, and thou with losing savest it.
But we will have a way more liberal
Than changing hearts, to join them; so we shall
Be one, and one another's all.

John Donne

NOTES

1. *Songs and Sonnets* (1557). Text Egerton MS. 2711. 2. *ibid.* Tex from same MS. (7) *grave*=engrave. 3. *ibid.* 4. *A Hundrea Sundry Flowers* (1573). 5. *The Paradise of Dainty Devices* (1576 6. *ibid.* Refrain emended by 1578 ed. (22) *by . . . of*] B. M. Add MS. 26737, Ault; *before have lived their time and* P.D.D. 7. *ibid.* 8 *A Gorgeous Gallery of Gallant Inventions* (1578). 9. *A Handful o Pleasant Delites* (1584). 10. *Brittons Bowre of Delights* (1591). Tex Rawl. Poet. MS. 85.

11. *The Phœnix Nest* (1593). (1) *pleasures*] *measures* Linton. 12. *ibia saunсing*=sanctus. 13. *ibid.* Possibly by Ralegh. 14. *ibid.* 15 *The Arbor of Amorous Devices* (1597). 16. *The Passionate Pilgrin* (1599). 17. *Englands Helicon* (1600). (25) *rathe*=early. 18. *ibia* Text from *Poems* (1619). 19. *ibid.* From *The Honourable Enter tainment* (1591). 20. *ibid.*

21. *ibid.* (28) *say*=fine cloth (42) *her swain*] Bullen; *my swain* E. H 22. *ibid.* Formerly ascribed to Constable. 23. *ibid.* 24. *ibid* 25. *Poetical Rapsody* (1602). 26. *ibid.* 27. *ibid.* A. W. may mean 'Anonymous writer.' (8) *untwined*] 1602; *entwined* conj. (9) *fined*= *refined.* 28. *ibid.* 29. *ibid.* (20) *gowns*] *downs* (1602). 30. *ibid.*

31. *ibid.* Possibly by Donne. 32. *ibid.* (1608). (16) *affection*] MS. Harl 6910; *their faction* (1608). 33. *Songs and Sonnets* (1557). Text from Egerton MS. 2711. Wyatt had been imprisoned in May 1534 and again in May 1536. 34. *ibid.* Text from Arundel MS., except for *careful* (11) and *ease* (14), which are both from Tottel. Written on the execution of Wyatt's friend and patron, Thomas Cromwell 35. *ibid.* (1) *soote*=sweet (4) *make*=mate (10) *smale*=small (11 *mings*=mingles. 36. *ibid.* (4) *chare*=chariot (11) *disease*=lack of ease. 37. *Astrophel and Stella* (1591). Text 1598. 38. *ibid.* (14 Do they call ungratefulness there a virtue? 39. *ibid.* 40. *ibid* (5) *prease*=press.

41. *ibid.* 42. *Arcadia* (1598). 43. *ibid.* 44. *Delia* (1592). This and the next sonnet may have been suggested by Tasso, *Ger. Lib.*, xvi.

14–15. *Cf.* Spenser, *Faerie Queene*, ii. 12. 45. *ibid.* 46. *ibid.* *Cf.* Tasso, *Rime Amorose*, lvii. 47. *ibid.* *Cf.* Tasso, *Rime Amorose*, lviii. 48. *ibid.* See p. 25. 49. *Diana* (1592). (2) *flee*] Abercrombie conj.; *fly* 1592. 50. Todd MS. (9) *enclos'd beheld*] *enclos'd, behold!* K.M.

51. Harl. MS. 7553. 52. *ibid.* 53. *The Tears of Fancie* (1593). 54. *Brittons Bowre of Delights* (1591). (9) *grey*] *Phœnix Nest; grief* B.B.D. (Desportes, from whom this sonnet is translated, has *gris*). 55. *The Phœnix Nest* (1593). 56. *Parthenophil and Parthenophe* (1593). 57. *A Century of Spiritual Sonnets* (1595). 58. *Licia* (1593). This is said to echo a poem by Gruterus. 59. *Phillis* (1593). *Cf.* Ariosto's "Non senza causa . . ." 60. *Ovid's Banquet of Sense* (1595). The first sonnet of "A Coronet for his Mistresse Philosophie."

61. *Amoretti* (1595). 62–65. *ibid.* 66. *Idea* (1599). Possibly showing the influence of Shakespeare's Dark Lady sonnets. 67. *Idea* (1605). 68. *Idea* (1619). 69. *ibid.* 70. *Aurora* (1604).

71. *Sonnets* (1609). Written fifteen or twenty years before. 72–84. *ibid.* 79. The last line is quoted in the anonymous play *Edward III.* 82. (9) Most editors emend *Made* to *Mad.* (10) Graves defends the reading of 1609, *quest, to haue extreame* (11) Graves defends the 1609 reading, *and very wo.* This is subtle, but scarcely fits the general argument of the sonnet. (13) The usual insertion of a semi-colon after *knows* spoils the point. 83. (14) *she*=woman. 84. (2) *Feeding*] *My sinfull earth* 1609. 85. *Poems* (1616). 86. *Flowres of Sion* (1623). 87–90. *Poems* (1633).

91. *Caelica* in *Works* (1633). The sequence was begun fifty years before, but the religious sonnets may have been written after Sidney's death. 92. *ibid.* 93. *Pandosto* (1694). The earlier editions are without this poem, but some lines of it were set to music in 1620. Greene may not be the author. 94. *Menaphon* (1589). See p. 29. 95. Puttenham's *Art of English Poesy* (1589). Sidney also wrote the poem in the form of a sonnet, but the shorter version is better. 96. *Rosalynde* (1590). 97. *ibid.* 98. *Greene's Mourning Garment* (1590). 99. *Greene's Farewell to Folly* (1591). (10) *music's*] *modest* Linton. 100. *Robert, second Duke of Normandy* (1591).

101. *Greene's Groatsworth of Wit* (1592). 102. *The Life and Death of William Longbeard* (1593). 103. *Piers Plainness' Seven Years' Prenticeship* (1595). 104. *Primaleon of Greece* (1596?). Text from

Englands Helicon. 105. *Observations in the Art of English Poesy* (1602
There were many attempts by Spenser and others to write u
rhymed lyrics in classical metres. This is one of the rare successe
106. *The History of Horestes* (1567). 107. *Campaspe* (1584). Te
1632. See p. 52. 108. *ibid.* 109. *The Arraignment of Paris* (1584
110. *Sappho and Phao* (1584). Text 1632.

111. *Two Italian Gentlemen* (1584). 112. *Galathea* (1592). Acted
1585. 113. *David and Bethsabe* (1599). Acted *c.* 1588. 114. *Mid*
1592). Text 1632. 115. *The Old Wives' Tale* (1595). 116. *ibi*
117. *The Hunting of Cupid.* A few fragments of this play are pr
served in the Drummond MSS. 118. *Summer's Last Will an*
Testament (1600). Acted 1593. 119–20. *ibid.* See *Love's Labour*
Lost and *The Two Gentlemen of Verona* for some of Shakespeare
early songs.

121. *ibid.* 122. *Mother Bombie* (1594). Text 1632. 123. *Old Fortun*
tus (1600). 124. *Patient Grissill* (1603). This song may be b
Chettle or by Dekker. See *As You Like It*, *Much Ado*, an
Twelfth Night for Shakespeare's songs of this period. 125. *ibi*
126. *The Shoemaker's Holiday* (1600). 127. *Histriomastix* (1610
Acted *c.* 1599. 128. *The Maid's Metamorphosis* (1600). 12
Cynthia's Revels (1601). 130. *ibid.*

131. *Blurt, Master-Constable* (1602). See *Hamlet*, *Measure for Measur*
and *Othello* for Shakespeare's songs of this period. 132. *Volpo*
(1607). 133. *The Rape of Lucrece* (1608). (16) *stare*=starlin
134. *The Woman-Hater* (1607). 135. *The White Devil* (1612). 13
Epicœne (1616). Acted 1609. See *Cymbeline*, *The Winter's Ta*
and *The Tempest* for Shakespeare's later songs. 137. *The Knig*
of the Burning Pestle (1613). 138. *Thetys' Festival* (1610). 13
The Two Noble Kinsmen (1634). Acted *c.* 1611. (9) *her bells*=
hairbells? 140. *The Maid's Tragedy* (1619). Acted 1611.

141. *The Masque of the Twelve Months* (1848). Some think this is
Collier forgery; but see *T. L. S.* December 15, 1950 and *N.*
March 29, 1952. The parallels with Chapman's Hesiod and h
known masque suggest that he was the author. 142. *The Capta*
(1647). Acted 1613. Two stanzas appear also in *The Knight of t*
Burning Pestle. 143. *The Mountebank's Masque* (1788). Text
emended by Ault from Bodley MS. Ashm. 36–37. 144. Byrc
Psalms, Sonnets, and Songs (1588). 145. *ibid.* (6) *chill*=I will (
wood=mad (22) *freezing*] Bullen; *freeze in* 1588. 146. *ibid.* Te

from MS. Rawl. Poet. 85. (12) *For why*=because. 147. Byrd's *Songs of Sundry Natures* (1589). 148. J. Dowland's *Songs or Airs.* 149. *ibid.* 150. Cavendish's *Airs and Madrigals* (1598).

151. Farmer's *First Set of English Madrigals* (1599). 152. Jones' *First Book of Songs and Airs* (1600). 153. *ibid.* 154. *ibid.* 155. J. Dowland's *Second Book* (1600). (13) *But in*] Ault; *But* 1600. (14) This line may be corrupt. 156. *ibid.* 157. *ibid.* (6) *though*] *thought* 1600. (9) *bedimm'd*] Chambers; *be dimmed* 1600. (15) *seeds*] Chambers; *sees* 1600. 158. Thomas Weelkes' *Madrigals* (1600). 159. Jones' *Second Book* (1601). 160. Rosseter's *A Book of Airs* (1601).

161. *ibid.* Translated from Catullus. 162–6. *ibid.* 167. Dowland's *Third Book* (1603). 168. *ibid.* (10) *them*] *it* 1603. (15) *will*] *wit* 1603. 169. Tobias Hume's *Musical Humours* (1605). 170. Thomas Ford's *Music of Sundry Kinds* (1607).

171. Jones' *Ultimum Vale* (1608). 172. Weelkes' *Airs or Fantastic Spirits* (1608). 173. Jones's *The Muses' Garden for Delights* (1610). 174. Corkine's *Airs* (1610). Text from Campion's *Fourth Book.* 175. *Two Books of Airs* (*c.* 1613). 176. *ibid.* 177. *The Third Book of Airs* (*c.* 1617). 178–179. *ibid.* 180. *The Fourth Book of Airs* (*c.* 1617).

181. *The Posies* (1575). (24) *peat*=pet. (26) *proyned*=pruned. 182. *The Shepheardes Calender* (1579). Elisa=Queen Elizabeth. (23) *cremosin*=crimson. (32) *yfere*=together. (56) *bellibone*=lovely girl. (63) *forswonk and forswat*=worn out and over-sweated. (84) *behight*=called. (99) *tawdry lace*=silk necktie. (102) *coronations*= carnations. (106) *paunce*=pansy. (107) *chevisaunce*=wallflower. (108) *flower delice*=fleur-de-lys. 183. *Hecatompathia* (1582). (1) *and days*] K. M., ; om. 1582. 184. *Verses of Praise and Joy* (1586). Written in the tower before his execution. 185. *Scylla's Metamorphosis* (1589). Trans. from Desportes. 186. *Polyhymnia* (1590) Possibly by Sir Henry Lee, about whom it is written.
187. *Astrophel and Stella.* Text 1598. 188. *ibid.* (1591). (24) *Dione*= Venus. 189. Alison's *An Hour's Recreation* (1606). Text MS. Rawl. Poet. 148. (*Cf.* Ault). 190. *Phillis* (1593). (19) *nill*=will not.

191. *St Peter's Complaint* (1595). 192. *ibid.* (1602). 193. *ibid.* (1602) 194. *Arcadia* (1598). 195. *ibid.* (21) *trentals*=a set of thirty requiem masses. Spenser's *Epithalamion* (1595) and *Prothalamion* (1596), two of the greatest Elizabethan lyrics, have been omitted for lack of space. 196. *Poems in divers humours* (1598). Text from

Englands Helicon, which omits some moralizing lines. 197. *Hymn of Astraea* (1599). The initial letters form the words Elisabeth Regina. 198. MS. Rawl. Poet. 85. 199. Chester's *Love's Marty* (1601). 200. *Epigrams* (1616). S.P.=Solomon (not Salathiel Pavy.

201. Scoloker's *Daiphantus* (1604). Written in the Tower whe Ralegh was expecting execution. 202. *Certain Small Poems* (1605) (11) *me there*] Beeching; *with thee* 1605. 203. *The Shepheards Siren* (1627). 204. *Cælica* (1633). Written in the sixteenth century. 205. *Poems* (1633). 206. *ibid.*

BIBLIOGRAPHY

Anthologies

ULT, N.: *Elizabethan Lyrics* (London, 1925).
ULLOUGH, G. and GRIERSON, H. J. C.: *The Oxford Book of Seventeenth-century Verse* (Oxford, 1934).
HAMBERS, E. K.: *The Oxford Book of Sixteenth-century Verse* (Oxford, 1932).

Editions

LLOTT, K.: *Poems of William Habington* (Liverpool, 1948).
RBER, E.: Thomas Watson's *Poems* (London, 1870). *Tottel's Miscellany* (London, 1870).
ARTLETT, P. B.: *The Poems of George Chapman* (New York, 1941).
OND, R. W.: *The Complete Works of John Lyly* (Oxford, 1902).
RETT, C.: *Minor Poems of Michael Drayton* (Oxford, 1907).
ULLOUGH, G.: *Poems and Dramas of Fulke Greville* (Edinburgh, 1939).
HARLTON, H. B., and KASTNER, L. E.: William Alexander's *Poetical Works* (Manchester, 1921–29).
OLLINS, J. C.: *The Plays and Poems of Robert Greene* (Oxford, 1905).
UNLIFFE, J. W.: Gascoigne's *Works* (Cambridge, 1907–10).
E SELINCOURT, E.: *The Poetical Works of Spenser* (Oxford, 1912).
ELLOWES, E. H.: *English Madrigal Verse* (Oxford, 1920).
RIERSON, H. J. C.: Donne's *Poems* (Oxford, 1912).
RUNDY, J.: *The Poems of Henry Constable* (Liverpool, 1961).
AYWARD, J.: *Donne, Complete Poetry and Selected Prose* (London, 1929).
EBEL, J. W.: Drayton's *Collected Poems* (Oxford, 1931–41).
ERFORD, C. H., and SIMPSON, P. and E.: Ben Jonson's *Poems and Prose Works* (Oxford, 1947).
ASTNER, L. E.: William Drummond's *Poetical Works* (Manchester, 1913).
ATHAM, A.: *Poems of Sir Walter Ralegh* (London, 1951).
EE, S.: *Elizabethan Sonnets* (London, 1904).

MACDONALD, H.: *The Phoenix Nest* (London, 1926). *Englan Helicon* (London, 1950).
MUIR, K.: *Collected Poems of Sir Thomas Wyatt* (London, 1949). *Unpublished Poems of Sir Thomas Wyatt* (Liverpool, 1961).
PADELFORD, F. M.: *Poems of Henry Howard, Earl of Surrey* (Seattl 1920).
ROLLINS, H. E.: *Tottel's Miscellany* (Cambridge, U.S.A., 1928–2
The Paradise of Dainty Devices (Cambridge, U.S.A., 1927).
A Gorgeous Gallery of Gallant Inventions (Cambridge, U.S.A., 192
A Handful of Pleasant Delights (Cambridge, U.S.A., 1924).
The Phoenix Nest (Cambridge, U.S.A., 1931).
Brittons Bowre of Delights (Cambridge, U.S.A., 1933).
The Arbor of Amorous Devices (Cambridge, U.S.A., 1937).
Englands Helicon (Cambridge, U.S.A., 1935).
A Poetical Rapsody (Cambridge, U.S.A., 1931–32).
SPRAGUE, A. C.: Daniel's *Poems and Defence of Rhyme* (Londo 1950).
VIVIAN, P.: Thomas Campion's *Works* (Oxford, 1909).
WALLER, A. R. and GLOVER, A.: *The Plays of Beaumont and Fletch* (Cambridge, 1905–12).
WILSON, M.: Sidney's *Astrophel and Stella* (London, 1931).
WOOD, H. H.: *The Plays of John Marston* (Edinburgh, 1934–39).

Criticism

DELATTRE, F., and CHEMIN, C.: *Les Chansons Elisabéthaines* (Par 1948).
ING, C.: *Elizabethan Lyrics* (London, 1951).
JOHN, L. C.: *The Elizabethan Sonnet Sequences* (New York, 1938).
JOSEPH, M.: *Shakespeare's Use of the Arts of Languages* (New Yor 1947).
PATTISON, B.: *Music and Poetry of the English Renaissance* (Londo 1948).
PEARSON, L. E.: *Elizabethan Love Conventions* (Berkeley, U.S. 1933).
SCOTT, J. G.: *Les Sonnets Elisabéthains* (Paris, 1929).
TUVE, R.: *Elizabethan and Metaphysical Imagery* (Chicago, 1946).
WHITE, H. O.: *Plagiarism and Imitation during the English Renaissa* (Cambridge, U.S.A., 1935).

INDEX OF AUTHORS

(Italicized numbers refer to pages of the Introduction; others refer to numbers of poems.)

INDEX OF FIRST LINES

(*References are to page-numbers and not to the numbers of the poems.*)